In Defense of Freedom

The Story of the Monroe Doctrine

On December 2, 1823, in a dramatic session of Congress, a message from James Monroe was read. In it he declared that our country would tolerate no further colonization in the Western Hemisphere by any foreign power. A milestone in our history had been passed, a decision made to preserve our hard-won independence. Often misunderstood, sometimes misused, changed and modified over the years, the Monroe Doctrine nevertheless stands as a vital symbol of our nation's deep commitment to the freedom of all men in all countries. In this book the author traces the course of historical events that made the Monroe Doctrine necessary and explains why its application over the years has been complex and controversial.

Books by Paul Rink

IN DEFENSE OF FREEDOM
The Story of the Monroe Doctrine

THE LAND DIVIDED, THE WORLD UNITED
The Story of the Panama Canal

In Defense of Freedom

The Story of the Monroe Doctrine

by Paul Rink

MAPS AND DRAWINGS
BY BARRY MARTIN

Julian Messner JM *New York*

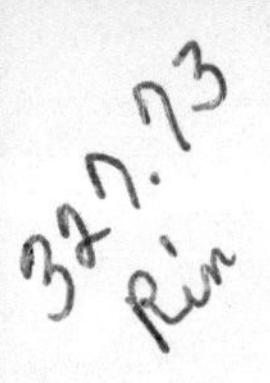

PUBLISHED SIMULTANEOUSLY IN THE UNITED STATES AND CANADA BY JULIAN MESSNER, A DIVISION OF SIMON & SCHUSTER, INC., 1 WEST 39 STREET, NEW YORK, N.Y. 10018.

PRINTED IN THE UNITED STATES OF AMERICA
LIBRARY OF CONGRESS CATALOG CARD NO. 68-14935

In Defense of Freedom

The Story of the Monroe Doctrine

James Monroe

FIFTH PRESIDENT

Inaugurated March 4, 1817—served until March 3, 1825

1

WASHINGTON, D.C., DECEMBER 2d, 1823.

Gloomy clouds pressed down on the rag-tag little city huddled on a low strip of land between the Anacostia and "Patawmack" Rivers. Leaden skies alternately dripped rain or swirling snow. A freezing winter wind flowed from nearby fields and forests, swept over the town, pierced the shivering people to the bone and did its best to congeal the mud and water of the streets to an iron-hard mass.

Crowds of pedestrians sloshed up Pennsylvania Avenue toward the government buildings which loomed on a small hill just beyond the grove of leafless Lombardy poplars planted by Thomas Jefferson. When the British burned and bombarded Washington just ten years before, the Capitol building had been saved from complete destruction by a lucky rainstorm. Except for the newly built wing of the Hall of Representatives, the structure was still a sorry mess of scorched walls rising from the mud.

The pedestrians ploughing grimly over the rough board sidewalks, or the foot-punishing stone chips salvaged during the construction of the President's House and then strewn over the paths, were mainly Congressmen—members of the House of Representatives. They were an insolent lot, suspicious of pomp and disrespectful of powdered elegance. They were unpolished men from farms, cities, seaports, from far-off clearings in green and quiet forests, asking nothing from any man—countryman or foreigner.

This morning these cocky "Yankee Doodles" lost no opportunity to demonstrate their independence, or their bad humor, as they stumbled through the ice and mud on the way to conduct the business of their government. They shook their fists, swore angrily and issued vulgar challenges at the carriages which swept past them, splashing them with freezing water. In these carriages rode the "quality" —a few wealthy people of the city, Cabinet members, elegant Senators, foreign Diplomats and their ladies.

One of these vehicles belonged to Baron Tuyll, Russia's Minister to the United States. The wigged, powdered and beribboned Baron was nearly hidden in the mass of furs he wore to keep out the cold. Sourly he stared out the windows at the Indian Queen Hotel, garish and untidy but still Washington's most elegant hostelry. From its tavern, men poured into the street, joining the crowd heading toward the Capitol.

In spite of the need to hang to the seat straps as the carriage bucked and pitched in the ruts, and in spite of the penetrating cold, Baron Tuyll found the time and energy to worry.

"President Monroe," he mused, "will never dare. Quite impossible to imagine such a public rebuke to the Tsar. A ridiculous custom anyhow, this State of the Union Message. Private correspondence between gentlemen is one thing; this is another."

Tuyll's glance swept disdainfully over the curious-looking citizens outside. They were dressed in everything from coonskin hats and deer-hide pants and jackets to rough homespun. Many of them carried long rifles and seemed to need baths and hair trims. Some appeared the worse from too much to drink.

"How," Tuyll asked himself, "is it possible that fellows such as these can take part in affairs of state? But they do. No getting away from it. Americans are an unpredictable lot—even President Monroe, though he seems something of a gentleman. Like every last one of them, though, he's got his head full of this democratic nonsense."

Baron Tuyll's musings were interrupted as the carriage of Stratford Canning, the British Minister, swept alongside. He composed the lines of worry on his face and bowed formally to His Britannic Majesty's representative.

Canning also had his worries, although he did not share Baron Tuyll's deep concern. Canning was an aristocrat, a gentleman in every sense of the word; nevertheless, he was more at ease in a world of democratic processes than that from which the elegant Russian had come. He too, however, had his private thoughts. "Will Mr. Monroe really dare? Can he really spurn the offer of the British Crown? Publicly? I can't imagine it. Too much is at stake."

As Canning stared at the gloomy wintry scene outside, at the swirling, turbulent throngs of people, he suddenly chuckled. "These Americans are such a damnably touchy and independent lot. One never knows what they will do."

His thoughts briefly touched on his colleagues from Russia, Spain, France and all the other countries of the Holy Alliance. Then he laughed outright. "I shouldn't be surprised. President Monroe just might dare. And if he does tell all of us in front of the whole world to go to the devil, it would surely deflate a good many of these pompous asses."

In utter weariness, James Monroe stared through the

windows of his study at the snowy scene outside. He was a big, powerful man, but this morning he was bone tired, more so than he could ever remember.

Monroe was sixty-five years old and had spent his entire life in public service. Wearily his mind traced back over the years. First the war, and the long grinding enlistment in the Revolutionary Army starting in 1776. He had left William and Mary College to enlist. Then victory and national independence at last but still no rest. There had been so many, many problems in those early days, with so few precedents for guidance, as Americans took up the business of governing themselves. Monroe had literally been drafted for one public post after another, all of them difficult and demanding.

The Virginia Legislature, the Continental Congress, the Constitutional Convention and the United States Senate had all taken their toll of his strength. Then had come years abroad as Ambassador to France and England, and again back home for service as Governor of Virginia. Finally, in the years prior to his election to the Presidency, Monroe had served first as Secretary of State and then as Secretary of War during the crucial times of President Madison.

When James Monroe took over the duties of President, in 1817, there were few men in the country more familiar with the affairs of the United States of America. He knew what his country needed. He knew what he wanted for it. He knew the hearts of his countrymen, and what they wanted. In spite of this tremendous knowledge, the decisions which had been thrust upon him the last few weeks had not been simple. Making them was not easy; he was torn and drained of strength.

Monroe gazed in somber contemplation at the last dark figures outside as they hurried through the snow to the Capitol to await his message. "Yes," he thought, "they all have a dream for themselves and for this country. And it's my dream too. But what strength could a dream have against the ships, the cannon, the soldiers of such empires as England, France, Russia, Austria, Spain . . . ?"

Monroe grimaced. His mind refused to continue adding up the awesome tally of European might. He knew better than most men what short work the power of a truly aroused Old World could make of the little United States and its scattered ten million people. Not for a moment during the past months had the awareness of the military strength of Europe left James Monroe.

Even the walls of the building where he lived reminded him. Originally constructed of Virginia freestone, the structure had been gutted and burned to a shell by the English in the War of 1812. It was now painted white because no amount of scrubbing could remove the stains of soot. From now on, the building would be called the "White House," instead of the original "President's House."

"Yes," he mused, "it's easy to talk of freedom and independence and . . ." Monroe shook his head sharply. The time for musing, for thought, for worry and fear was past. The decisions had been made and he had no regrets. Specific notes covering specific situations had been delivered to Russia and England. All that remained now was for the broad and final statement to be given publicly.

He walked to a small table by the door—a beautiful, graceful table he had bought in Europe years before. On the dark mahogany lay a sheaf of papers. This was his Message on the State of the Union. One more small decision remained, and he had to make it now.

George Washington and John Adams had delivered their Messages to Congress in person. Thomas Jefferson and James Madison had not done so, preferring to let a clerk read them. Which should he do? Certainly there was no tradition as yet for Monroe to follow. Personally he believed that Messages of great importance ought to be delivered by the Chief Executive himself. But . . . he shrugged . . . did it really matter? Right now he was too tired to face the packed hall, and it was on this basis that he made his decision.

Monroe picked up a quill pen, dipped it in ink and scratched his name at the bottom of the last page. As he did this there was a knock on the door. He opened it to face his secretary and a messenger from the Capitol.

"Sir," said the messenger, "Congress is assembled. Will you read your Message, or will the clerk do so?"

"The clerk." Monroe put the papers in an envelope. The secretary sealed it and gave it to the messenger, who securely strapped it in a dispatch bag. The man saluted, turned and with long, hard steps strode down the hall. In a moment he was gone.

Monroe walked slowly down the hall after him. His glance swept over the furnishings, the lovely pictures and tapestries. After the fire, Congress had been niggardly about buying new things, so nearly all the furniture had been carefully chosen by Monroe and his wife, Elizabeth, and paid for out of their own pockets. They intended to give these things to the White House, but this winter morning of 1823, there was no way of knowing if they would survive, or even if the United States of America would survive.

The Hall of Representatives was packed to the rafters. In the spectators' galleries, diplomats, country squires and prosperous businessmen rubbed elbows with plain, run-of-the-garden citizens. Below them, on the main floor, Representatives lounged, "whittling and spitting," making rude remarks or gazing insolently upwards at their "betters."

Throughout the hall there was a continual coughing and blowing of noses and clearing of throats. In spite of the roaring fireplaces, and the puffing, new-fangled Franklin stoves, the place was cold. There wasn't much anyone could do about the weather or the ills that came with it. Coughs, colds, sniffles and sore throats were accepted as facts of life during the winter. They were taken in stride and all grouped together as fevers, or "the ague."

Over the noise and conversation could be heard the droning voice of the clerk as he read Monroe's statement. The audience was bored with the greater part and made no effort to conceal it. To these early lawmakers, their own affairs—hunting, shipping, the whale-oil trade, farming and the like—were much more important matters than the state of the Army or Navy or Post Office. Nor was anybody much interested this morning in the evils of the slave trade, the deplorable condition of the Cumberland Road or the proposed canal to connect Chesapeake Bay with the Ohio River. Neither were Monroe's feelings about the Greeks, who were in revolt against the Turks, or his sentiments on privateering subjects of much concern.

Everyone was pleased, however, and there was a moment of quiet as the clerk read that the government was operating in the black and that at the moment there was a surplus of about nine million dollars in the treasury. The Representatives, to a man, nodded in approval. Let no one forget that *they* controlled the purse strings.

As the clerk read on, though, the chatter rose in volume. Much as everyone present might be interested in the finances of the country, there was one other matter which interested the people this morning, and until their curiosity was satisfied, they could not be quiet. They talked of this matter, and it alone, among themselves.

A small man, pale, in city clothes, spoke to his neighbor,

a giant, spar-shouldered young fellow dressed in the outfit of a shipmaster. "Is it true," he asked the sailor, "that the Tsar of Russia has said the whole Pacific belongs to him?"

"Aye, Sir, he has said that. And do you know, he has a tidy little colony only eighty miles from San Francisco to back up his claim. I saw it with my own eyes the last time I was in the Pacific after sea otters."

"But who cares what happens on the Pacific coast?" The speaker was a spare, flint-faced lawyer from New England. "It must be three thousand miles away."

"The Congressman from Vermont should come home with me," another man said. He was tall and lean and dressed in homespun. His eyes were gray and quiet, with a look in them that could have come only from gazing at far horizons. "The Pacific coast is not so far. Home in Tennessee, it seems you can almost see it. The plains and the mountains and the valleys go on and on, but it's all America—clear to the ocean. It's our continent."

It's our continent. The words had a fine ring. The little group fell silent, and the clerk droned on and on.

Then the frontiersman spoke again. "And it isn't just the Russians. I hear too much about this Holy Alliance in South America. And the French and the British. Can't they ever leave us alone? Do we have to fight them all? All over again?"

"Fight 'em all, would you?" asked the sea captain. He shook his head dubiously. "I don't know. You've got your troubles along the Gulf and along the Mississippi all right, but we've got 'em too on the high seas. I've seen too many of those big, fast frigates. Nothin' but cannon lookin' at you. I don't like 'em."

"Tom, if I didn't know you better I'd think you were afraid," said the lawyer-Congressman from Vermont. "I don't want another war any more than the next man, but sometimes there's nothing left to do but fight."

"I know, I know," grunted the sailor. "You're right. But a war won't do us any good. Too much else needs doing."

A nearby listener leaned over and said quietly, "But if it keeps us free, we'll face it and it'll be worth it."

There was a chorus of affirmative answers.

The clerk read on, but as Monroe finally wound up his comments on the Greeks and the Turks, everyone in the hall sensed the Message was at last coming to the point.

"Will he dare tell 'em off?" the sailor asked of no one in particular.

The Tennessean shrugged. "Why not? He's an American, isn't he? Same as Washington and Jefferson and old man Adams, and all the rest of 'em. They risked their hides all right and didn't ask too many questions when they started this country fifty years ago. Sure he'll tell them off."

As if in answer, the clerk reached that part of the Message that everyone had come to hear. And he did "tell 'em off."

In several cogent, widely spaced paragraphs Monroe spelled out exactly what his countrymen wanted for America. In precise, clear language he laid down the gauntlet to England, Russia and the entire Holy Alliance.

Hardly breathing, the crowd drank in the words: "The occasion has been judged proper for asserting, as a principle in which the rights and interests of the United States are involved, that the American continents, by the free and independent condition which they have assumed and maintained, are henceforth not to be considered as subjects for future colonization by any European powers."

There was much more as Monroe elaborated. He said America would not interfere with present European colonies in the Western Hemisphere but stated that these colonies were not to be expanded. He insisted the country would stay out of European politics and expected Europe to stay out of those of the New World. He proclaimed the belief that other American states must be allowed to work out their own destinies and warned Europe to let them do so.

The Representatives and the crowds in the galleries could scarcely believe their ears. The savage tigers that stalked the jungles of world politics had been warned off, and more than this was the thinly veiled promise that the pygmy—the United States of America—would use arms if necessary to see that they stayed away.

There was a long moment of stunned silence; then the people in the hall burst into wild cheering. Canning, the British Minister, stole a quick glance at his esteemed diplomatic colleagues, took in their consternation and then burst into laughter.

Ask a dozen different people what the "Monroe Doctrine" is and you'll get a dozen different answers. They'd all probably be wrong. The Doctrine isn't a law, an official manifesto or a proclamation. It isn't an official government document. It is simply a speech!

The thoughts which it expressed, however, have endured and have taken on the power and the majesty of law itself. And for just one reason: they reflected at the time, and down through history since that time, to the present day, what was in the hearts of the American people.

Any one of them, our forefathers, shivering that morning in the winter of 1823, might have paraphrased Monroe's elegant language with simpler, earthier words, but the meaning would have been the same. "If they'll leave us alone, we'll leave them alone. If they *don't* leave us alone, watch out."

Behind those words was a dream of liberty for themselves and for all men—a belief in the right of a man to govern himself, to work out his own destiny. It was a statement that we would respect this wish in others but that we would also expect others to respect this wish in ourselves and in the hearts of all the other peoples of the nations in the New World.

Why did Americans feel it necessary to express themselves in such manner at this time? Why did such sentiments develop in the United States? The reason is the story of the Monroe Doctrine. The threads are long and tangled. They spread over half the world, and they take us further back even than the birth of our own national freedom.

2

A SMALL SAILING SHIP bore down out of the black, stormy waters of the North Atlantic toward the coast of America. It tumbled and swooped in sickening dives. The noise of the crashing seas, the creak of timbers and the roar of wind in the rigging were deafening.

The group of people standing near the rail of the vessel gazed grimly at the rocky and forest-clad coast which loomed ahead of them. This was North America, their new home. Europe lay thousands of miles and many weeks' travel behind. The year was 1700. These men, women and children talked little, but what they said was from the heart.

"So that is it," muttered one of the men gazing at the land, which was coming up swiftly now.

A companion leaning on the rail nearby shook his head dubiously. "It truly does seem cold and inhospitable, Jim," he said, "and yet so beautiful."

"And it will remain beautiful," said the woman standing beside Jim, her husband. Her thin clothing was no protection against the wind and cold spray, and she shivered, trying to arrange her shawl more comfortably and to keep the jacket buttoned on the little boy who clung to her hand.

"Yes, Mary, I am sure it will be," answered Jim. He smiled.

"Indeed, Mary, you *are* right," mused still another. "And beautiful because we shall be free."

"Won't there be a King any more?" asked the little boy.

"Of course we'll have a King, same as in England—and the lords and all the others. All this land belongs to England, and so do we." The boy's father gazed with pride at his son and then smiled. "But *here* it's going to be different."

"Aye, so it will be," murmured others in the group.

Jim's glance swept over the land—the gray rocks, the forests, the high cliffs. His jaw hardened. "We're poor. We owe money. Half of us are little better than bound slaves. We have nothing but our backs and our two hands, but we'll use them. And life *will* be better for us. Any of us will be the equal of any other man because of what he *is* and not because of that to which he was born."

"And what about the likes of that one?" asked his friend, nodding imperceptibly toward the stern of the vessel, where a well-fed, warmly dressed individual chatted lightly with the Captain. "What will he do? What will he find here? Why is he even here except to boss us? He is rich, and I want no more such men pushing me about." The words were almost hissed.

Jim laughed. "Dick, even *he* will be different in this new land. Not much perhaps, but enough. Yes, even *that* one will learn to stand on his own. This continent will never be tamed by people who must depend on the sweat of others."

Dick still glowered. "This may very well be. But I tell

you, I shall not be pushed too hard. I have been driven like an animal too long. I want to be let alone to do what I can for myself and this brood here." His glance swept swiftly over his wife and band of shivering children huddled about her. "And I *shall* be let alone—by him and anyone else who thinks he is better than I."

Dick flexed his back and his arms. He was a powerful man; his drive and his strength flowed from him. Already he seemed to be grappling a continent.

"Right, Dick," echoed several other men and women. "We are with you." The children looked with frightened eyes at their elders. Never before had they heard talk like this.

Jim laid his hand on the shoulder of his friend. The bone and muscle were hard with determination. He said, "And I too, Dick. We are done with oppression. Never shall we drive any fellow man with whips and swords, nor shall any man drive us again. We are done with oppression."

The word "oppression" is a common one these days, but it describes a situation most Americans know little about. This was not the case with those who first settled North America. These early immigrants had lived on very intimate terms with oppression.

The Europe of those times seemed to have run out of steam. Its land was tired. Governments, peoples and religious and economic orders bubbled in a foul stew—unable to go forward, reluctant to let go of the past. However, there were hidden but strong currents of powerful ideas whispering—elusive but clear. What these ideas said to men's souls and minds was enticing.

They whispered that life did not have to be as difficult and pain-filled as it was. They said that a man had worth and dignity. They said he had a right to suggest how he would be ruled, a right to refuse to have to fight somebody else's war, a right to worship any god he chose, to run a business or a farm if he so desired and to use part of the profit of his toil for himself and his family. In short, in Europe the idea of freedom was stirring.

Such thoughts were extremely dangerous to those in power. The "divine" royal families, the clergy, the aristocrats who owned the land and the rich bankers who owned the money had no desire for change, and they fought the new ideas with all their strength. Greater cruelty, harsher laws and increased oppression of every kind made life ever more miserable.

The plight of the common people—the "cattle," as they were called—swiftly worsened as the kidnappings, starvation, massacres, hangings and public whippings multiplied by day and night. There was no hope of resistance because these humble ones could not get weapons, or if they could, did not know how to use them. They had to either hide or flee. North America was one of the places to go, and many came, bringing little with them but the hope that life would be different, better.

And, miraculously, it was better. The very nature of existence in this rough, raw land made it so. A man was more of a man, more self-reliant, more dependent upon himself. The power and the arrogance of total authority were still there, but they were less absolute. The gap between rich man and poor, between bound apprentice and master, was still there, but it was less pronounced than it had been in Europe—not much, but enough to give hope for true freedom.

As time passed, the hope flowered. A strange and intoxicating ferment gripped these early settlers in America. They were discovering a new and heady thing—opportunity. They were swiftly becoming aware of the great and sweet power which lay within themselves. As the years passed, in spite of the politics and the very harsh economic conditions in the colonies, people found that it was possible to *make* their lives better if they were willing to work hard at it.

Since the time of the very first European colony in the Western Hemisphere—that on the island of Santo Domingo, established by Columbus in 1493—the peoples of both North and South America had been involved in the squabbles of their motherlands. Europe's wars and her miseries overflowed in abundance to her children across the sea. But as these children grew and reached maturity, their resentment grew. They seemed to know instinctively that they were creating a whole new order of existence, unlike anything the world had ever seen before. They also knew that this could never be done except in an atmosphere of freedom.

The desire for freedom first reached fighting pitch in North America in April of 1775. The demand for liberty was a pretty cocky demand for people still subject to the mighty crown of England, but once it had started, there was no going back. The taste of freedom was too sweet; the yearning for independence became overpowering and the colonies plunged into the future with the Declaration of Independence on July 4th, 1776.

After the war had started, the attitude of the American colonists was expressed best of all by Tom Paine, a feisty little printer who lived in Pennsylvania. Paine had been born in England in 1737, the son of a Quaker corset-maker. Early hardships (and they were many) made him sympathetic and understanding of the poor and unfortunate—of all the victims of oppression. He came to North America in 1774 because of the urging of his friend Benjamin Franklin. Immediately he started on a publishing career, ultimately writing emotional and powerful arguments for American independence.

In his most famous article he said, "I challenge the warmest advocate for reconciliation to show a single advantage which this continent can reap by being connected with Great Britain . . . but the injuries and disadvantages which we sustain by that connection are without number; and our duty to mankind at large as well as to ourselves, instructs us to renounce the alliance; because any submission to, or dependence on, Great Britain, tends directly to involve this continent in European wars and quarrels and sets us at variance with nations who would otherwise seek our friendship; and against whom we have neither anger nor complaint. . . . It is the true interest of America to steer clear of European contentions, which she can never do, while, by her dependence on Britain, she is made the make-weight in the scale of British politics."

Alas for such brave words. The American people and their "out at the sleeves" armies of patriots soon found it was one thing to defy Britain on paper and quite another to do so on the battlefield. As the war dragged on, it took, finally, the ghastly retreat to Valley Forge and the near breakup of the Revolutionary Armies to convince the people and the Continental Congress that the struggle was practically lost unless there was outside help. Where to turn? Hateful as the idea was, there was only that from which America was trying to free herself—Europe.

One of the most sophisticated and worldly men of those days was Benjamin Franklin, at the time the American representative in France. Congress commissioned him to enter into negotiations with the French Government, and Franklin must have shuddered when he read the instructions.

Naïvely, they made no mention of the hateful word "alliance" or of any other commitments which such a treaty would normally include.

Franklin, of course, felt the same way, but he did not delude himself. He transcended his instructions and negotiated a treaty which was acceptable to the French. It bound the two nations to make peace and war together and in other ways went far beyond the innocent hopes of Congress. In the realization that it was the best that could be done under the circumstances, the American Government approved. Thus it was that at the very outset of existence the United States of America was forced to enter into a hateful and binding alliance with a foreign power. However distasteful, there was no choice. The country was fighting for its life with its back to the wall.

The war continued amidst great suffering and strong resentment at what seemed paltry French aid. By 1780, however, the fortunes of the Revolutionary Armies were on the mend. Americans were learning how to fight the British. They avoided head-on confrontations with English troops and instead organized swift-moving bands of deadly, sharp-shooting guerrillas. These chopped away steadily at the fringes of the enemy, gradually wearing away its strength.

The cautious but brilliant tactics of George Washington and his elusive "mountain generals," including Nathaniel Greene and Daniel Morgan, finally broke the back of the British offensives in the interior of the country. Such battles as King's Mountain, in the Carolinas, and Cowpens and Guilford Court House so mauled the English that they were forced to retire to the seacoast to lick their wounds and await further developments behind their fortifications.

By then, more effective French aid had arrived in America. George Washington and the Comte de Rochambeau combined their American and French forces and marched

United States
North Atlantic Ocean
Gulf of Mexico
TROPIC OF CANCER
West Indies
MEXICO
CUBA
DOMINICAN REPUBLIC
JAMAICA
HAITI
PUERTO RICO
BR. HONDURAS
Caribbean Sea
GUATEMALA
HONDURAS
NICARAGUA
Central America
EL SALVADOR
PANAMA
COSTA RICA
VENEZUELA
GUIANA
SURINAM
FR. GUIANA
N
COLUMBIA
EQUATOR
ECUADOR
PERU
South America
BRAZIL
BOLIVIA
Pacific Ocean
PIC OF CAPRICORN
ARGENTINA
CHILE
URUGUAY
South Atlantic Ocean
Lands of the Monroe Doctrine

to Yorktown, Virginia, where the Marquis de Lafayette had the British, commanded by General Cornwallis, under siege. With the help of a French fleet under the Comte de Grasse, they forced Cornwallis to surrender on October 19, 1781. The war was over.

The treaty with France was like gall to Americans for years to come. President after President squirmed and twisted and through various interpretations, some of them quite far-fetched, tried to get out of it. Nevertheless, most Americans recognized the debt they owed to France and, like George Washington, believed that nations as well as individuals should keep their word. The country tried to live honorably with its agreement; but as time passed, the task became more and more difficult.

At the end of the War of Independence, an awesome array of problems—domestic and foreign—faced the faltering little collection of former British colonies. Resolving them would have been difficult for a long-established and powerful nation. That the country was able to walk safely through the dangerous tangles of international politics was a high tribute to the quality of the people and their government.

Many of these problems came directly out of the fiercely growing determination of Americans to be left alone to develop their country as they saw fit. This burning urge to be left unmolested and to molest no one was nowhere better expressed than in John Adams' diary when he commented on a conversation he had had with the British peace negotiator at the end of the Revolutionary War. He wrote: " 'You are afraid,' says Mr. Oswald today, 'of being made the tools of the powers of Europe.'

" 'Indeed I am,' say I. 'It is obvious that all the powers of Europe will be continually maneuvering with us, to work us into their real or imaginary balances of power, while they are weighing out the pounds . . . but I think it ought to be our rule not to meddle, and that of all the powers of Europe, not to desire us, or perhaps, even to permit us to interfere in their business if they can help it.' "

In connection with this desire of the American people to be left alone, one important characteristic of a democracy became quickly evident: frequently the instincts and wishes of the masses of the citizens were far ahead of those of their "leaders." America's early leaders discovered this.

Even that clear-eyed believer in the common people, Thomas Jefferson, had something to learn in this respect. Jefferson knew well, and respected, the common American's simple faith: "Leave us alone and we'll leave you alone." He shared it, and yet, when he was Minister to France in 1785, he actually developed a plan in which America would join in a virtual alliance with several European governments.

The Barbary Coast was that section of North Africa along the Mediterranean stretching from Egypt to the Atlantic Ocean. It was called "Barbary" because it was inhabited by a fierce and warlike desert people, the Berbers. Today we know these lands by the names of Tunisia, Algeria, Morocco and Tripoli. At the time of Jefferson's venture into international treaty-making, no ship—American or any other—was safe from the ferocious pirates who sallied out from the various Barbary strongholds to prey upon vessels foolish or unlucky enough to stray into these waters.

Jefferson had proposed that America join forces with a number of European nations in a military expedition against the sea rovers, but these nations had turned him down cold. They had no intention of allying themselves with the brash little country on the other side of the Atlantic. The snub still smarted as Jefferson sat in his apartment in Paris mulling over the matter.

"Yes," he muttered to himself at this backhanded reminder of the feelings of his countrymen at home, "they are so right. It is utterly futile ever to expect anything constructive from these Old World monarchies." And then he laughed outright at himself. "And what a narrow escape *you've* had. Think of the hue and cry if such a treaty had been submitted to Washington." He shook his head in astonishment at his own foolishness. Then he picked up a pen, dipped it in ink and started composing a letter to a friend in America. Humorously he wrote, "Were I to indulge my theory, I would wish the United States to practice neither commerce nor navigation, but to stand with Europe precisely on the footing of China. We should thus avoid all wars and all our citizens would be husbandmen."

Others—among them John Jay, an early American patriot—did not get off so lightly as Jefferson. Jay learned his lesson while he was Secretary of Foreign Affairs under the Confederation in 1785.

One of the most pressing problems to face the young nation as it struggled to get on its feet was that of expansion westward. Since the days of the earliest settlements, people had lived with their eyes and their hopes pointed toward the West. Many hardy souls had plunged into the unknown forests and always brought back the same tales—tales of a vast continent, fertile, virgin and beautiful beyond anyone's dreams. Except for roving Indians, it was empty and waiting. It was a land where a man and his family could stand or fall on their own strength, on the sharpness of an eye over the sights of a long rifle or the willingness with which an ax might be swung.

When independence finally became a reality, courageous men, women and children began to load their wagons and head for the mountain passes. The Cumberland Gap was one of the early roads which carried these migrants. What kind of a civilization they would eventually establish was anybody's guess, but the idea of movement was in people's hearts and relentlessly urged them on. They just wanted to *go*—why or where nobody really could have said.

Long before Americans had dreams of building a great nation, before even the fact of independence, they had considered themselves "continentals." Even before the remotest thought of filling a continent, the Army was a "Continental" Army. Money was "Continental" currency. The early Congress was a "Continental" Congress.

The big obstacle to early mass migrations was the mighty Mississippi River and the endless miles on each side of it—all owned and controlled by Spain. Spanish policy toward all her New World possessions was a very simple one, and from the time of the landing of Columbus it had been enforced with brutality and blood: everybody keep out.

The suspicions of Americans regarding foreign entanglement did not apply to commercial matters. The people wished to trade where and how it pleased them. In line with this, John Jay was instructed to negotiate a treaty with Spain which would grant Americans trading privileges. How naïve were Jay and the government.

The Spanish diplomats granted the commercial rights to Jay but also insisted on a political and military alliance which demanded that, among many other things, the United States guarantee all Spanish borders as they existed in the New World—a tall order!

Jay agreed and then quickly learned a thing or two about his fellow Americans. When word of the proposed treaty was made public, there was such an outburst of anger that it was never even submitted to the Senate for ratification. Americans would find other ways of trading on the Mississippi without involving themselves in Spanish political problems.

Besides Jay, there were other backers of the luckless

treaty who were exposed to a strong taste of what the citizens of the United States really had in mind when they said "no foreign entanglements." One of them was the confidant of James Madison and Thomas Jefferson, a young Congressman named James Monroe. He apparently would have accepted the mutual border guarantees if the price had been the right of navigation on the river instead of trade rights only. Thus, the future author of the Monroe Doctrine was also taught a lesson as the sentiment of the American people about isolationism slowly hardened into official government policy.

Another of the great problems which faced the country in these years was that of strengthening the Federal Government. The old Confederation simply would not work, and in the great debates at the Constitutional Convention in Philadelphia in 1787, the isolationist temper was very clear.

The treaty-making power of the President required a two-thirds approval vote of the Senate. This was a very high figure and was due partly to the anger and the distrust which people still felt over John Jay's willingness to enter into an alliance with Spain over trading rights on the Mississippi.

This distrust of the people and their dread of foreign influences were also reflected in the terrible battles at the convention over just how strong the Federal Government should be. Those who battled so forcefully for "states' rights" did so because they were afraid of the "entanglements" which a strong central government might force upon them. And, ironically, the arguments for overcoming this problem would have created a weak central government that could be overcome by aggressive foreign powers. As the Constitution was finally worked out, it was a compromise—a strong Federal Government which could act with speed and decision but which would also be subject to the control of the people.

A further and really vexing problem continued to be the despised treaty with France. By 1788 this had gone so far that in conversations with France's Minister in Washington the Secretary of State mentioned that this ten-year-old treaty had been entered into for the sole purpose of helping Americans win independence and that now, surely, the treaty had lapsed. How naïve America was!

The reply from Paris was immediate and emphatic. "You will correct the ideas of Mr. Jay," the French Minister was instructed. "You will assure him that the King regards his alliance with the United States as unalterable. . . . This is a doctrine which you ought to develop and which the King's Council is surprised to see so little understood."

Like it or not, America would have to live with its first foreign alliance.

So, with much fumbling and many false starts, the early leaders of America, and the public, were building a fence around the country. The fervent wish was that it would keep people out of their affairs and keep Americans at home minding their own business. America had enough problems without picking up additional ones across the oceans.

Across these oceans, however, events not of the New World's doing were moving swiftly. As the 1780s came to a close, the Old World exploded in a burst of war and terror. The catalyst was provided which would propel America at a full run into the future, and eventually leave it with the "no trespassing fences high and strong.

The catalyst was the French Revolution. It and its repercussions were to dominate America for years to come. The stirring words of America's Declaration of Independence were the immediate flame which inspired the French revolt against traditional authority. For the first time in the history of man, somebody had done something about the thrilling concept that the power of a government must stem from those which it governs. The American Revolution and the final establishment of a free, democratic United States proclaimed to the whole world that this idea of government need not be mere words—it could work! Liberty, and justice and brotherhood were possible goals for courageous men to achieve.

The seeds for the enunciation of the Monroe Doctrine were planted in early America by the very nature of life in the New World. They sprouted out of the soil of the French Revolution.

3

MOBS RAN WILD through the streets of Paris. Guillotines were kept razor-sharp, and cobbles ran red with blood as an absolute monarchy and an extravagant, arrogant aristocracy expired.

As the drama unfolded, the French Revolution spread outward until most of Europe was engulfed in a gigantic, nightmarish bath of blood. This was to go on for twenty-five years.

The reigning families of Europe were at first inclined to joke at the predicament of French royalty. The King of France had in recent years been too difficult and demanding for even his fellow monarchs to stomach. Also, the disturbances were at first regarded as local and minor. Any king worthy of the name should know how to deal with the unarmed rabble raging through the streets of Paris. Order surely would soon be restored.

Soon, however, even the most blind could see that this was no mere discontent to be put down by a few well-timed cavalry charges. Then the unthinkable happened. The mobs laid hands on "God's anointed." Louis XVI and his Queen were beheaded. The liquidation of the entire French nobility seemed an ominous possibility. The kings and queens and all the members of the ancient and intricate structure of European aristocracy came to a chilling realization.

The basic power of these old, hereditary, ruling families came from the belief that the right to govern had been conferred by God himself and that an act against them was pure heresy. If this heresy could be committed in France, it might very well happen in other countries. Whether the King of France was popular in royal circles was one thing; an act of heresy against the elect was another. So the thoroughly alarmed monarchs of Europe began gathering arms and mustering soldiers. France and the French people were not to be allowed to get away with it. They had to be punished if all these royal heads were to be saved and if the principle of the divinely granted power of kings was to be preserved.

As the tides of retaliation began to swell outside France, the plight of the French people was not helped by the convulsions taking place within their own borders. The nation writhed in an agony of spilling blood as the terror grew. Radicals fought with conservatives. Lower classes battled the middle classes. They all enthusiastically ferreted out and murdered any member of the upper classes they could find. As each revolutionary government rose, and fell, it left an ever-increasing gory legacy of blood and butchery to those which followed.

On one point, however, all these governments were in complete agreement. They might be willing to tear French society to pieces from top to bottom, but they also realized that the armies gathering outside to strike at France had to be crushed somehow, or the entire revolution would fail. Furthermore, many important men believed it was France's sacred duty to export revolution to all oppressed subject peoples, all over Europe.

So, for many reasons, France embarked on a long and very painful series of foreign wars. These various reasons were quickly forgotten, however, and were supplanted by the sheer desire for conquest. Never, in any people, at any time in history, did the flame of *pure conquest* ignite more quickly or more fiercely than it did in the French after their revolt from the monarchy.

Republican armies fought in the Netherlands, in Austria, Spain, Italy, in far off Egypt. Various nations and coalitions fought against them, including such ultrapowerful antagonists as Prussia, Austria, England and Russia. A thoroughly alarmed Europe finally managed to unite and to bring the rampaging French to a halt and force them back into what seemed natural borders.

The continent heaved a sigh of relief. These war-hungry monarchs of Europe, though fired with the desire to revenge themselves against the French and to put an end to this democratic nonsense, had had enough. They hoped fervently that France would settle down now, even though she was a hated republic, and put her house in order. This was the hope, a hope for peace in 1799.

Alas for the hopes. A new star rose over the tired peoples of Europe, and the color of this star was blood-red. Its name was Napoleon Bonaparte. Bonaparte was an obscure Corsican Corporal, driven by a lust for power and glory, and through a display of personal magnetism and sheer military genius seldom seen in man's history, he had risen to command French Republican armies and finally to be crowned Emperor of all France.

As soldier, General and First Consul under the various Republican governments, and then finally as Emperor,

Napoleon led his fanatically loyal and battle-hardened armies on a career of conquest unheard of in modern times. In superbly brilliant maneuvers on battlefields with names which still ring down the years of history—Zurich, Marengo, Austerlitz, Jena and many, many others—he destroyed the forces of the different coalitions which rose against him.

By 1802 most of Europe was Napoleon's. Effective opposition had been crushed. Proud nations such as Austria were soundly beaten, humiliated and forced to sue for peace. At the peace conference held in Amien, the continent was carved up to suit the French. There was only one nation left with the resources to challenge Napoleon—England. France was master of Europe, but England was still mistress of the seas.

The two exhausted enemies glared at each other across the English Channel. For the moment they needed time to regather strength. England could not think of attacking Napoleon by land, and the French Navy was helpless before the guns of the British fleet. Napoleon laid futile plans for an invasion of England, and the British did their best to reorganize their prostrate allies on land.

The final showdown was still more than twelve years away, but in the meantime there was no real peace. The Treaty of Amiens was scrapped by 1803 (it had lasted just a year), and once more Europe armed to try and rid itself of the scourge of Napoleon. Austria, Russia, Britain, Sweden and others, singly and together, over the years gave fruitless battle to the French. The tramp of millions of marching men and the rumble of cannon echoed from one corner of the continent to the other. In spite of efforts of the French to build a powerful navy, the British retained control of the sea. Famous victories, such as that of Lord Nelson at Trafalgar, ensured that the ability of the English to fight could not be broken and that Napoleon would have to abandon his dream of invasion across the Channel.

Feeling in America about the French Revolution was deeply divided at first. Some honorable men, conservatives such as Alexander Hamilton, viewed the rampaging violence with deep mistrust. Others, James Madison, James Monroe and Thomas Jefferson—all men with an abiding faith in the common man and his ability to govern himself—joined multitudes of common Americans in pleasure at the overthrow of French ruling classes.

In general, though, events across the Atlantic were remote. Regardless of emotional sympathies, America had her own problems. Down to the last man, Americans thanked God they were not involved in the storm in Europe. As the grisly drama progressed, with ever-increasing havoc and destruction, they and their government considered themselves thrice blessed to be out of it. There was nothing vague about the isolationist sentiment now. The determination to keep clear of Europe was official and popular.

Wise John Adams, in his second annual Presidential address in December of 1798, had said bluntly, "To the usual subjects of gratitude I cannot omit to add one of the first importance to our well-being and safety—I mean that spirit which has arisen in our country against the menaces and aggressions of foreign nations."

But the position of neutrality and of noninvolvement was not an easy one. The problems were enormous, and one of the greatest was still the old one of the alliance with France. The possibilities for calamity because of it were incredible. France, for example, had colonies in the New World. Was the United States bound to defend them? Was she also bound to declare war on France's enemy, England? She also had New World colonies, strong and well armed. Little wonder Americans redoubled efforts to get out of the treaty.

M. Genêt, the Minister sent by the revolutionary government of France to demand that America enter the war against England, conducted himself with such appalling arrogance that even those who might have been sympathetic were repelled. On the other hand, the English fleet, and troops along the Canadian border, were equally arrogant and high-handed in their disdainful treatment of Americans and their property. The country was wedged between the devil and the deep blue sea. France was dangerous, but mighty Britain even more so. Neutrality became the watchword of the American people and the official policy of their government. They wished to become a nation of traders and merchants and, if possible, to make an occasional bit of profit from the contestants!

Even Thomas Jefferson, the staunch and vocal believer in democracy, was repelled by the fury in Europe. The French monarchy had been overthrown. This was all to the good. Napoleon had not yet proclaimed himself Emperor, but the Republican governments showed themselves to be even more brutal and conquest-bound than the monarchy had been! Jefferson, however, joined his countrymen in wishing to trade with the battling nations. In total cynicism he was moved to comment, "Since it is decreed by fate, we have only to pray that their soldiers will eat a great deal."

When John Adams succeeded Washington as President in 1797, his first task was to reopen negotiations to try and free America once and for all from the treaty with France. The talks dragged on and on. The outrageous demands of the French hampered progress at every turn. At one time they actually suggested to the Americans that with bribes they might buy release from the treaty!

Adams wisely laid this entire correspondence before the American people. When it was published, there was such an outcry that the nation was practically engaged in an undeclared, informal war with France. Feelings ran so high that many people demanded the country ally herself with England and attack those Spanish Latin-American colonies which by now, because of Spain's defeat by France, were under French rule.

Adams would have no talk about any alliance with Britain, but he did use, and play hard upon, the "informal" war with France. The result, finally, was a treaty signed in 1800, which ended the "war" and terminated the alliance. By 1801, when Thomas Jefferson was elected President, the country was free of all foreign commitments and more united than ever to see that matters stayed this way.

However, there were many times when the position of noninvolvement was extremely difficult to maintain. Out of sheer necessity and because of the extremely complex world situation, the United States had to embark on ventures not to her liking and to toy with the idea of treaties which also seemed inspired by dire need.

For example, the faltering Spanish monarchy had ceded the entire Louisiana Territory to France when Napoleon came to power. Napoleon quite obviously had plans for extending his empire to the New World, to both North and South America. Americans watched with horror as he began to take steps.

One of his first moves was to send an expedition under General Le Clerc to subdue the rebellious former French colony of Haiti. Because of malaria and yellow fever, because the mulatto officers in the French Army were suspicious that Napoleon intended to restore slavery in Haiti and because of the fanatical determination of the former black slaves on the island to remain free, the venture was a failure.

Napoleon next turned his attention to New Orleans. His

plan was to establish it strongly as a first move toward tight French control over the entire vast Louisiana Territory. If Spain had been bad as a neighbor, the thought of Napoleon taking active possession of Louisiana was downright horrifying to Americans. Spain was weak, her great days gone; the same most certainly was not true of France.

President Jefferson had little love for the British but he had far less for Napoleon, and so he actually toyed with the possibility that some sort of an alliance with England against France might be necessary. Writing to a friend he said, "On the day that France takes possession of New Orleans, we must marry ourselves to the British fleet and nation."

To try and stave off what seemed to be an impending crisis of enormous proportions, Jefferson sent James Monroe and Robert Livingston to Paris to make an offer to the French to buy outright the "island" of New Orleans. They were very much in luck. For reasons of its own, France was willing to discuss not only the sale of New Orleans island but that of the entire territory of Louisiana. Perhaps even Napoleon realized that this was a time which was only a breather and that he would soon have his hands full in Europe again—much too full, in fact, to bother with the development of huge colonies in America.

Such a prospect had not even been considered when the American emissaries set out for Europe. They had no instructions to cover this new situation. Furthermore, there was no chance at all of any help from home. Months would go by before word could get across the Atlantic and back.

Monroe and Livingston ended up by doing what any thrifty agent would do when shopping for real estate and suddenly presented with a whopping bargain. They snapped it up. With a scratch of the pen they bought the Louisiana Territory and doubled the size of the United States. The date was December 20, 1803.

As Robert Livingston signed he is reported to have said, "We have lived long, but this is the noblest work of our whole lives. . . . From this day the United States takes its place among the powers of first rank."

Napoleon, too, had a prophecy to make about the result of the sale of Louisiana to the Americans. "This accession of territory affirms forever the power of the United States, and I have just given England a maritime rival that sooner or later will lay low her pride."

The price of the enormous territory was over twenty-seven million dollars. It was cheap. America heaved a giant sigh of relief. The country was free of problems with Spain or France or anyone else in the vast tract of land that stretched from the Gulf of Mexico to Canada and from the Mississippi to the Rockies.

America was growing in size and strength, not only on land but also on sea. Since 1785, when, as Minister to France, Thomas Jefferson had made his ill-conceived effort to induce various European nations to join the United States in a naval venture, he had been itching to do something about the Barbary pirates. Now, in 1804, shortly after Louisiana had been purchased, and during his first term as President, Jefferson saw his opportunity. The naval action which he set off took place thousands of miles from the United States, and it illustrates forcibly the growing power of America and the firmness of the policy which it could now pursue regarding dangerous, but necessary, foreign ventures.

The Mediterranean night was soft and thick. No moon gleamed in the sky. Only the pale light of stars illumined the decks of the warships ghosting under shortened sail over the swells.

Alongside one of the vessels, a longboat was moored. It was deep and heavy with kegs of gunpowder, fuses and rags soaked in oil.

A whispered command was given on the quarterdeck of the frigate.

Men with blackened faces clambered down the towering wooden side of the ship and took up their oars. The last one in was Stephen Decatur, a young lieutenant in the very young United States Navy. He took his place at the tiller. The longboat was shoved off.

"Man your oars. 'Way together."

The heavily muffled oarlocks made not a sound as the boat glided over the swells toward Africa. The ghostly white sails of the warships were engulfed in the night.

This fleet was blockading the Barbary Coast. From the ports of Algiers, Tripoli and Tunis swarms of swift and bloodthirsty pirates sallied forth to plunder the ships of the United States, or those of any other nation foolish enough to venture near. Alone, America had decided that enough was enough. These savage predators had to be wiped out.

Decatur steered his boat by the stars and by dim landmarks on the smudge of coast. As the boat crept into Tripoli harbor, he kept to a course that would take him around the barriers across the entrance and through a very narrow channel which passed directly under the muzzles of cannon in the forts ashore. Decatur relied upon the sooty blackness, and stealth, to get him safely inside.

An indistiguishable wraith, the boat slowly crept along, hugging the shoreline where the shadows were deepest. At last, safely past the grim fortress, Decatur took bearings as best he could and then headed for a long sandbar which jutted out from the beach. A heavy black shape took on the contours of the United States frigate *Philadelphia*.

Several days before, after tremendously heavy fighting, the *Philadelphia* became caught in a flat calm. Currents swept her ashore and ran her fast aground, helpless, on the sandbar. The pirates had swarmed out from shore like hornets, overpowered the crew and captured the vessel. Such a powerful warship could not be left in enemy hands, and it was Decatur's desperate mission to try and destroy her.

" 'Vast heaving," came the whispered order. The longboat drifted near the *Philadelphia.*

"Ship your oars." Without a sound the Americans drifted closer and finally touched the rising hull of the stranded ship.

Like cats in the darkness, the barefooted sailors clambered aboard and quickly overpowered the sleepy guards, who had thought themselves secure behind the cannon at harbor's mouth.

In silence but with sure haste, Decatur and his "commandos" distributed the explosives strategically about the vessel—below decks, in the cabins, in the hold, in powder magazines.

A spark was struck. A soft flame, pale and yellow, glimmered in the darkness. Fuses sputtered, powder trains hissed. The sailors piled down the sides of the ship and pulled away as quickly as possible.

Behind them the warship erupted in a gigantic fountain of flame and smoke. In the confusion, Decatur and his crew made a miraculous escape to the open sea, where they were picked up by their own ships. In the entire action only one man was wounded.

Up to this point in 1804, the United States of America had been so weak it was unable to take a truly firm stand on much of anything. The acquisition of the fantastically huge Louisiana territory changed this. Now America was the undisputed power in the Western Hemisphere. Sending warships to the Mediterranean and destroying the *Philadelphia* spelled this out for the whole world to see and ponder.

If America wished to let people alone and in turn wanted to be let alone by them, it now had the population, the resources and the muscle to give real meaning to the wish. The desire to be allowed to work out the destiny of the nation in tranquility had long existed in the hearts of the people. Slowly but surely this desire had hardened into official government policy. Now, at last, there was power to make the policy stick.

In a very real sense the formal position of isolationism dates from the time of the Louisiana purchase in 1803. All that remained was a set of events or circumstances which would make that position or policy clear-cut and definite before the eyes of the whole world. Much needed to happen, however, before America's feeling about freedom for its own citizens and for all men in the Western Hemisphere would be spelled out publicly.

This moment was still in the future, twenty years distant. But the events leading to it were moving inexorably, and like the sequence of acts in a play, they unfolded. The cues for the actors came from Europe.

4

BY 1803 the thunder of war and its accompanying horrors rose once again across the Atlantic. These Second Napoleonic Wars were to bring many problems and difficulties to America, crossing the administration of President Jefferson and then, starting in 1809, that of James Madison. Both men devoted an enormous amount of time and effort to maintaining American neutrality. These efforts were successful, and the country walked a sure, if delicate and twisting, path which kept it out of direct warfare in Europe.

However, even in those relatively slow-moving times of the early 1800s, the earth was not small enough for any power—even one as unimportant as the United States—to remain completely untouched when the rest of the world was engulfed in a hurricane. So it was that in a roundabout way, during Madison's administration, the nation became involved in the War of 1812, sometimes called the Second War of Independence.

The early years of the resumption of the war between France and England were prosperous years for neutral American shippers and merchants. They traded with both belligerents, but as time passed and the position of the warring nations became more desperate, this trade became increasingly hazardous and difficult.

By 1807, a series of edicts and counteredicts from each side made commerce well-nigh impossible.

Said England: "No trade except through England." This meant that American ships carrying goods to France had to stop first in British ports and pay British duties on their cargoes.

Said Napoleon: "No trade through England." And this meant that American ships bound for France would be confiscated by the French if they had passed through English ports en route.

These edicts had teeth in them and were enforced ruthlessly, leaving little choice for the Americans. If their ships sailed directly to France they were liable to interception and confiscation by British blockaders. If they touched first in England and then went on to France, they could be confiscated by the French.

The American Government did everything in its power to stop this trade, but in spite of its wishes, over and over again hardy sailors and ships took the terrible risk. Britain was literally fighting for her life and retaliated with all the power of her great navy. Time and again American ships were stopped. Only the most strenuous efforts kept the United States from outright war over these violations of its neutrality and the private rights of its citizens.

Arrogance of the British on the high seas in the matter of the impressment of Americans also brought the two countries close to war a number of times. The British Naval Service was a hard one, and the Royal Navy had long recruited seamen where and how it could for enforced duty. America could not object as long as this brutal practice was carried out against English subjects on English ships or soil.

But when the British took upon themselves the right to stop American ships and seize alleged British subjects, or alleged deserters, it was another matter. The rough-and-ready methods by which British officers questioned the allegiance of sailors on American ships, and removed them in chains to the nearby warship, was a direct and ruthless violation of American sovereignty and neutrality. In addition, there was no appeal of any kind from this impressment. Along with British subjects thus seized, many Americans inevitably were taken, so the country was in a constant turmoil of anger over the matter.

The whole thing came to a head when the heavy British frigate *Leopard* actually fired upon the American frigate *Chesapeake* and forcibly removed four seamen. In this attack upon a public vessel of the United States, British arrogance had gone too far. There was such a clamor in America that the English eventually had to make amends.

Thus the country pursued its precarious but peaceful pathway. Nevertheless, war finally did come. The real reasons for it, however, were not commercial disputes or disputes over neutrality on the high seas. They lay much deeper.

Although the country had just acquired the enormous Louisiana territory, Americans were still not satisfied. Their yearnings went clear to the Pacific and to Florida, areas still held by Spain, and to the north as well, to Canada, which was English. The old dream that the entire continent was destined to be American would not die. The more rabid expansionists, called War Hawks, felt that there was no time like the present to take the Stars and Stripes to the most distant reaches of North America.

These War Hawks were young, fiery men, mainly from western and southern states. Led by such famous patriots as Henry Clay and John C. Calhoun, they regarded England as the country's arch-foe. They bitterly resented the humiliations to which the United States had been subjected on the high seas. More important, though, was their anger against the British because of what they considered English opposition to American expansion westward.

The War Hawks may have been right. Since the loss of the original thirteen colonies, and with complete logic from her own point of view, England had tried in every way possible to halt the American movement to the West. This opposition had taken many forms. One of the most dangerous for Americans was the British policy of supplying arms in great abundance to hostile Indian tribes. British agents, for example, supplied guns and ammunition to the Shawnees under the famed Indian chief Tecumseh, who inflicted a terrible defeat on the frontier army under General William Henry Harrison at Tippecanoe.

Little wonder that the War Hawks raised the cry that only by throwing the English out of Canada could there ever be any peace or security on the continent. They also hoped that a war with England would give America the opportunity to seize Florida from Spain, which was a British ally at this time.

After a seven-month debate in Congress, President James Madison was finally pushed to declare war in June of 1812. He did so over the very strong opposition of conservatives from New York and the New England states.

During the lengthy and violent argument when the country was making up its mind about whether or not to go to war, Congress had done nothing to strengthen the Army or Navy or to lay plans for raising the necessary funds. The whole subject was highly unpopular in many sections of the nation, especially in the manufacturing and shipping states of the east. These areas were well aware that the heaviest burden of taxation to finance the struggle would fall on them because of their industries. They were also resentful of the fact that long and patient negotiation had finally resulted in the repeal by Great Britain of the hateful edicts which had fostered the trade restrictions and the impressment of sailors on the high seas. Owing to the slowness of communications and the general hysteria whipped up by the Hawks, this fact became known too late to prevent the declaration of war. So high did the antiwar feeling run in Massachusetts, there was actually talk of treason and secession from the Union. The talk came to nothing, but it did serve to set this section of the country apart from the rest of the nation for a long time.

July 18, 1812. The sea off the coast of New Jersey was a glassy, flat surface, glinting under the rays of a sun shining from a cloudless, windless sky.

The peaceful scene was shattered by the steady cannonade from the ships floating on the ocean. A large British fleet, its white sails limp, tried in vain to reach an American vessel some distance ahead of it. All the cannonballs fell short of their target.

The American ship, the frigate *Constitution,* moved sluggishly over the sea. In its rigging sailors poured buckets of water over the canvas to try and hold the slightest puff of wind. Ahead of the ship, six longboats, manned by sweating, panting oarsmen, desperately tried to keep the *Constitution* out of British gun range. Slowly the huge vessel, four hundred and fifty feet long and weighing two thousand two hundred tons, crept over the water. There was no sound but the heavy breathing of the men and the bark of the coxswains as they called a cadence.

The *Constitution* had been trapped by the strong British fleet, but then pursued and pursuers alike were caught in the flat calm. Confidently the English prepared to wait it out. With the coming of wind they expected to blow the American ship out of the water. However, they had overlooked the determination of their former colonists. The Americans promptly lowered their boats and by superhuman efforts dragged their beloved *Constitution* out of gun range. When the wind finally came, the ship was far enough ahead for it to crack on all sail and escape the trap.

A month later, on August 19, the tables were turned.

Captain Isaac Hull of the *Constitution* studied the towering white mass of sail coming up over the horizon. At last he put his long glass down.

"Man battle stations," was his only comment.

The ship approaching was the British frigate *Guerriere,* approximately the same size and carrying the same weight of cannon as the *Constitution.* This time, with odds even, there would be no running away.

"Will she give battle, Captain?" asked a lieutenant.

Hull looked at the young man and smiled grimly. "They'll carry the battle to us every inch of the way," he said. "Great Britain did not become mistress of the seas by manning her ships of war with men who refuse battle."

And indeed the *Guerriere* did not refuse. Arrogantly she bore on, her topmasts aswarm with sharpshooting marines, her great black cannon primed and ready, secure in the legend of English naval invincibility.

Soon the two ships were within range. Puffs of smoke billowed from the English ship. Splashes of water rose in fountains about the American, short of her and beyond, as the gunners probed the distance. Captain Hull of the *Constitution* gave further orders.

"Fire at her rigging; at her top hamper." He grunted as the shots from the other vessel became louder, more accurate "But hold your fire until I give the word."

The *Constitution* sailed steadily onward, the serenity of

her appearance, with her swelling white sails and majestic hull, at odds with the tension within her. All hands looked toward Captain Hull. How long would he hold his fire?

At last he said, "Commence fire." The word was passed to the lieutenants in charge of the batteries. "Fire!" they cried. Fuses sputtered. The long cannon roared, leaping back and forth, tearing at their restraining tackles. The sweating gunners swabbed, loaded, primed, aimed, fired. Excited boys, the "powder monkeys," raced between the guns and magazines. So rapidly did the cannon fire, they could scarcely keep up with the cry for powder.

The *Constitution* erupted in a volcano of fire and steel. The ship and the men in her had memories of humiliation, of long waiting, of thwarted national pride to spur them, and now they shattered the myth of English naval superiority. Within thirty minutes the *Guerriere* was a wallowing hulk, every mast down and without a shred of sail to steer by.

A few minutes later a boat danced over the waves to the *Constitution,* and Captain Hull accepted the sword of the English Captain in surrender.

During the height of the battle, according to legend, an American sailor saw British cannonballs pound hard against the oak of the *Constitution*'s hull and fall harmlessly into the water. "Hooray and hooray for 'Old Ironsides'!" he shouted in jubilation. And "Old Ironsides" it was, from that day to the present. The *Constitution* escaped the fate of her sister-ships and was not broken up when her fighting days were over. In 1927 she was completely rebuilt with funds donated by American schoolchildren. Today she may be seen in all her glory, a commissioned ship in the United States Navy, at her berth in Boston, an enduring monument to American fighting ships and the sailors who man them.

Except for such shining victories as that of the *Constitution,* there was little in the progress of the War of 1812 to give consolation to Americans. No doubt the War Hawks and other superpatriots had counted on England's mortal involvement with Napoleon to give the United States an easy victory. Or perhaps they had deluded themselves into thinking that America of those days was truly a world power.

They could not have been more wrong. England showed herself perfectly capable of fighting Napoleon on the seas and on a dozen bloody European fronts, at the same time finding ships and men enough to hold America at bay with her left hand. On top of this, the United States was woefully unprepared for war with anyone, let alone Great Britain.

Defeat followed inglorious defeat. The country was very nearly finished off before it even got started. According to the hopes of the War Hawks, the invasion and occupation of Canada were supposed to be the prime objectives. Attempts to enter Canada and capture forts along the border were complete fiascoes. Elsewhere the situation was just as bad. Occasional small victories for the Americans gave the country heart to go on.

Naval victories like that of the *Constitution* over the *Guerriere,* and that of Commodore Oliver Hazard Perry on Lake Erie in 1813, where he completely routed the British ships, spurred America to keep up the struggle. In fact, the small American Navy was the main source of inspiration that caused the country to buckle down. American ships gave an excellent account of themselves wherever they could find single enemy vessels, or squadrons small enough that they were not overwhelmingly outgunned.

American resistance began to stiffen, but in no sense did the war go well. The British actually were able to sail right up the Potomac River, land marines and burn half of Washington! They were finally brought to a half-halt at Baltimore. During this campaign the brave battle put up by the garrison at Fort McHenry inspired Francis Scott Keyes to compose the "Star Spangled Banner."

The war effort continued to harden as the people realized they had better get down to serious business or there would be real trouble. A number of small victories on land helped but did little to resolve the war.

One of the reasons for America's increased efficiency in the conduct of the war was the appointment of James Monroe as Secretary of War. The future author of the Monroe Doctrine did his best to secure a fighting command but instead was placed in the Cabinet. His daring, his courage, his enthusiasm and his optimistic faith in the American people are nowhere better illustrated than in dispatches written just before the battle of New Orleans. To the various governors in that area he wrote: "Hasten your militia to New Orleans. Do not wait for the government to arm them; put all the arms you can find into their hands; let every man bring his rifle; we shall see you paid."

On January 8, 1815, the British under Lt. Gen. Sir Edward Pakenham landed at the mouth of the Mississippi. They were defeated with tremendous losses by Americans under the command of General Andrew Jackson. This battle of New Orleans was fought two weeks after peace had been declared, but communications were so slow that word did not arrive in time to stop the fighting.

The peace treaty was signed in Ghent, Belgium, on December 14, 1814. The peace talks were brought about indirectly through the good offices of the Tsar of Russia, who offered to mediate. America was more than ready for peace! The small victories on land had been of little consequence when considered as parts of a long, unsuccessful war. The Navy had done well, but there were simply too many ships and cannon against it, and by war's end the entire coast was under tight and effective blockade. And worst of all for the future, the European campaigns against Napoleon were over, and regiment after regiment, thousands upon thousands of disciplined, battle-hardened British veterans of these wars, was landing in Canada preparing to attack America.

American negotiators came to the peace table with not one single demand. They merely asked a return to the situation as it had been. The English presented a formidable list of demands but ultimately were persuaded to drop them. The treaty fulfilled not one single objective for America but nevertheless was hailed with joyous enthusiasm. Even the Hartford Convention in New England received the news with joy, and the talk of secessionist proposals and amendments to the Constitution was dropped.

All during the war, with its reverses and disheartening ups and downs and with the dissatisfaction and discontent of the people, there had never been a single suggestion that the country turn anywhere for help. During the blackest days, when the possibility was real that the country might be overwhelmed, it would not have been unreasonable that the government might even have sounded out Napoleon for aid in fighting the mutual enemy, Britain. There had not been one word; the continued growth of isolationist sentiment and fear of the turmoils of Europe had grown too strong. Americans were utterly disillusioned. They apparently were willing even to go down in defeat, had it come to that, before entangling themselves again in the problems of the Old World.

Some of the effects of the War of 1812 were good for America. The country was driven back on its own resources. It learned to make good use of what it had, and the determination that the continent was going to be opened and developed by Americans was bolstered. There was no doubt that Americans were surely headed for the Pacific, whether Britain or anybody else approved.

The war also helped the people to unite and work as a unit, as a single, undivided nation. It gave them more confidence in themselves and in their destiny. And at the same time they learned that the nation must be strong. Pious statements of isolationism, of neutrality, were meaningless without muscle to back them up. Nobody was going to leave America alone just because the people preferred it this way. Reorganization of the Army and Navy followed the Peace of Ghent. Misfortunes and near disaster had taught the country a bitter lesson, and it was strengthened from it.

Napoleon had finally met defeat at Waterloo, a little village in Belgium, on June 18, 1815. The coalition armies which won the famous battle were headed by the Duke of Wellington and Marshal Blucher. Their victory may very possibly have been the most crucial in the history of mankind. The whole world heaved a great sigh of relief. After twenty-five long years, there was peace once more on earth.

America, too, relaxed, busy with a multitude of problems at home and secure in its growing strength. The country was filled with gratitude for its blessings, buoyant and optimistic as it moved into the future.

Since 1803 and the burning of the *Philadelpphia* in Tripoli, the infamous Barbary Coast had continued to be a festering sore and danger for shipping. Numerous expeditions by America's small but valiant Navy had helped, but the problem still existed. Tribute was still demanded and collected by the pirates. Accordingly, in 1815 Stephen Decatur was given command of a squadron of nine warships, and he sailed directly into Algiers harbor. He captured the Algerian flagship and pounded the forts ashore with his heavy cannon.

The Bey was given the choice of surrendering on American terms or outright war. He chose to surrender, and the matter of piracy, depradations and tribute was settled once and for all.

When Decatur returned home, a great banquet was held to celebrate the event. He rose to pledge a toast. Out of his overflowing heart he expressed his love, and that of all his countrymen, for America.

He said, "To our country! In her intercourse with foreign nations may she always be in the right. But our country, right or wrong!"

5

AT THE SAME TIME that the Napoleonic Wars were making a slaughterhouse of Europe, another tremendous series of events was reshaping the New World. Its effect on America and on the development of the Monroe Doctrine was greater than anything that had yet happened. It was an indirect stepchild of our own Revolution and a direct offspring of the French Revolution.

This was the revolt from Spain of Latin America. This revolt, more than any other single event in history, triggered the official public statement of the principles of the Doctrine. It pointed up in crystal-clear terms that the West—both North and South America—had concerns, a way of life and a democratic ambition totally different from those of Europe.

For centuries, Spain's policy toward her colonies had been one of cruelty and oppression. The New World possessions were regarded as gigantic treasure chests to be looted of gold, silver or whatever agricultural products could be coaxed by slave labor from the plantations. Natives were treated with incredible cruelty and were either killed outright or worked to death as slaves. The colonies were given no chance to develop on their own. No trade was permitted between Latin America and any other country but Spain. Foreign vessels were denied entry to the ports.

One of the bitterest pills for the colonists to swallow was that children who happened to be born in the colonies were considered inferiors and were treated as such. They were called Creoles, which means servant or child. They were never appointed by the Spanish crown to any official posts except the most minor, empty of authority.

Wealthy colonists went to great lengths to avoid placing this stigma on their children. If it could be afforded, a wife would make the long and hazardous trip home in a galleon for the express purpose of being on "Spanish" soil when the expected child was born, thus making certain the baby would be a "real" Spaniard and not an ill-fated Creole.

From its own shortsighted and narrow point of view, the Spanish crown was wise. These Creoles, born and reared in Latin America, could naturally be expected to have some feeling for the land of their birth and to resent being considered unfit or second-class citizens. So Spain took no chances. The entire colonial government was kept in the hands of appointees who came directly from the mother country and whose loyalties could not be questioned. The practice, however, ran a vicious circle. The constantly arriving new officials inevitably had children of their own, and unless the trips back to Spain could be managed, these children joined the ranks of the Creoles! This conflict between the American-born Spanish and the "true" Spanish officials finally brought matters to a head. All that the restless Creole populations needed was an opportunity, and they got it as a direct consequence of the French Revolution.

An interesting curtain raiser, which took the same pattern as the big revolts in South and Central America a few years later, occurred in 1791 on the island of Hispaniola. Hispaniola had originally been conquered and settled by the Spanish. As usual, the native population was very quickly exterminated by savage slavery and overwork, and Negro slaves were imported.

French buccaneers settled the western part of the island in such numbers that in 1697 this section was ceded to France and renamed San Domingue, though more frequently known by its native name, Haiti. The French continued to import Negroes, so that by the time of the revolution, the population consisted of about 32,000 white Frenchmen, 24,000 free mulattoes and the astonishing total of 500,000 Negro slaves.

The inspiring slogan of the French Revolution was "Liberty, Equality and Fraternity," and somehow the half-million Negro slaves in Haiti got the idea that these noble sentiments applied to them. Finally, in 1794, the Republican Government of France decreed emancipation. The trouble, however, was just beginning.

A few years later, in 1801, a former slave named Toussaint L'Ouverture, who had a decided flair for military matters, proclaimed national freedom, drafted a constitution and named himself governor for life. L'Ouverture was a native of Haiti and completely self-educated. He had a long background of successful warfare against the Spanish on the other half of the island and was one of the great patriots of the Caribbean. The blacks followed him in war and peace and obeyed his orders without question.

By this time Napoleon was running France to suit himself, and he had no intention of abandoning Haiti to a former black slave. He sent the expedition under General Le Clerc to crush the regime of Toussaint L'Ouverture.

In his efforts to establish a farflung ruling dynasty in Europe, Napoleon appointed many of his relatives as kings and queens over the lands he conquered. Thus his brother was King of Naples and later King of Spain. A sister, Elisa, was at first Princess of Lucca and Piombina and then Duchess of Tuscany. Another brother, Luis, was King of Holland. Another sister, Pauline, Napoleon's favorite, was married to General Le Clerc and accompanied her husband on the expedition to Haiti. Pauline was exceedingly beautiful, but vain and frivolous, and she created a deep and hated impression on that unhappy island. She led a pampered and luxurious life in a huge castle while the common people starved about her in the countryside.

At first all went well with Le Clerc's expedition. Toussaint was captured by trickery and sent in chains to France, where he died in the gloomy dungeons of Fort de Joux in 1803. One of the best generals in Le Clerc's army was Alexandre Petion, a Haitian mulatto. He fought well and fiercely for the French, but finally, convinced that Napoleon intended to restore slavery, he defected and joined the native forces.

After long and bitter fighting, aided by arms furnished by American merchants, the insurrectionists forced the French to a showdown. Le Clerc was dead of yellow fever. His army was thinned by this and other diseases as well as by battle losses and desertions. The French were all evacuated home, including Le Clerc's widow, the beautiful but shallow Pauline Bonaparte.

Haiti was now free of European domination but by no means free of war or tyrants. Devastating civil wars erupted, especially between the mulatto Petion, who was trying to organize a republic in the south, and Henri Christophe, a Negro general who proclaimed himself king in the north.

Christophe was one of the great dramatic and tragic figures of his time. An ex-slave, he was deeply suspicious of anything even part white, and this included the mulatto General Petion. The struggle between these two men was long and inconclusive and was ended only by Petion's death.

Petion was liberal and progressive and did his utmost to bring order to his country. Christophe was said to be half mad, filled with hatred and delusions of his own grandeur. He forced his subjects to work like animals building roads and harbors, all the while maintaining himself with tyrannical pomp in a huge, castle-like citadel perched on a mountaintop near the sea.

The glittering show and ludicrous magnificence of his court are easy to imagine today as one inspects the ruins of his castle or of his famous palace, Sans Souci. Christophe took his own life in 1820 because, according to some, his heart was broken at the failure of his ignorant, primitive people to live up to the hopes and dreams he had for them. Christophe is famous in legend and story; he was the inspiration for the widely known play "Emperor Jones," written by Eugene O'Neill.

Opportunities for revolt came a short time later to Spain's colonies, and they too were outgrowths of the French Revolution and the final assumption of power by Napoleon.

In 1810 Napoleon invaded and conquered Spain, deposing its ineffectual king, Ferdinand VII. Immediately committees and local governments were formed from one end of Latin America to the other. The purpose was to preserve the Spanish colonies intact until Ferdinand could be restored to his throne.

The unrest of the Creoles, however, was far to deep for them to be content for long with such a situation. They were restless with the desire for freedom. The example of the United States of America to the north was always with them. Liberty *was* possible if men could find the courage and the means to challenge the armed might of oppression. Nowhere on earth did the winds of freedom blow more seductively than they did in Latin America. Napoleon gave the Creoles their chance. Even though he had dreams of a great French empire in the New World, his hands were full at the moment. Furthermore, Spain lay helpless under the French Army and could not react effectively against revolt in her colonies. Inevitably the committees which had been organized to keep the empire intact for King Ferdinand took another direction. What at first had been a movement inspired by loyalty to the motherland became an outright struggle for independence.

By 1811 this new direction was clear. The royalists and the Spanish garrisons found themselves locked in a death grip with Creole revolutionaries. Because of the geography of Central and South America—impassable mountains, jungles, endless plains, swamps—this struggle broke up into several different efforts. Each took up arms for freedom more or less independently, under different leaders and banners.

Since the time of the earliest Spanish conquests, various revolts of oppressed native peoples had taken place. These revolts had all been put down by savage massacre and butchery. As the curtain went up for the final act in the drama of Latin-American independence, once again and for the last time Indian populations rose against their oppressors. The scene this time was Central America—Mexico.

Father Miguel Hidalgo, a Catholic priest who was in trouble with the Spanish Inquisition because of what they called his "heretical library," was deeply sympathetic with the oppressed situation of the Mexican Indians. He plotted with them, incited them to revolt and soon was at the head of a howling, savage army of more than 60,000. His scarcely controllable mob stormed throughout Mexico, killing and looting with a fury which had been bottled up for centuries.

The date on which Hildalgo formally opened the rebellion, September 16, 1810, is Mexico's Independence Day.

This horde of wild savages was at first looked upon with great satisfaction by the Creoles, but after the storming and subsequent massacre of the population of the town of Guanajuato, this elation changed to dismay. The Indians were bent on revenge and slaughtered Creoles and Spaniards alike. In the face of this common peril, the Creoles and the "peninsulares"—that is, the home-grown Spanish—managed to forget their differences. They joined forces against Hidalgo and in 1811 captured and shot him.

Immediately the Indian army was taken over by another "warrior-priest"—Father José Maria Morelos, a man who had great ability as a soldier and administrator. He brought the wild Indians under control, and most of Mexico came under his power. Declaring the country independent and free, he set up the beginnings of a liberal government. It didn't last long. In 1815 a Royalist Army defeated Morelos, and he met the usual fate of unsuccessful revolutionaries: a firing squad. The nation was once more in the hands of those loyal to the crown of Spain.

When Napoleon was defeated in 1815, King Ferdinand VII was restored to the throne in Spain. He was, however, so ineffectual that by 1820, progressive groups in Spain forced him to issue a constitution. Superreactionary and loyal groups in Mexico would have nothing to do with this semiliberal constitution which Ferdinand had proclaimed. They raised another army, put Agustin Iturbide in command and announced that its purpose was to defeat the remnants of the Indian armies which were led by Morelos' heir, Vicente Guerrero. The real purpose, however, was to free Mexico from the hated constitution.

These complexities were simple compared to what came

next. Iturbide betrayed his reactionary backers and joined forces with Vicente Guerrero and the Indians, and the two of them announced Mexico's independence under a modern and liberal constitution.

Thus Mexico's revolt from Spain went full circle. The revolt of Indians under a radical Roman Catholic priest was defeated by ultraconservative royalists afraid of a too liberal Spanish monarchy. They, in turn, were betrayed, and Mexico won final independence under an adventurer out to achieve his own ends.

The whole province of Central America now declared its independence from Spain and was annexed to Mexico. This vast district, called in those days the "Captaincy-General of Guatemala," extended clear to the Isthmus of Panama. After a few years it proclaimed its own independent status and, in spite of strong efforts to keep it united, broke up into the small, separate countries we know today.

In South America the movement for independence began a few years ahead of that in Mexico. It started not as a revolt of the Indian population but as a true rebellion of Creoles.

The "father of independence" in South America was a Venezuelan-born Creole. Francisco de Miranda was a superb example of the finest men produced in the New World Spanish colonies. He was handsome, intelligent and well-educated and had an international reputation as a soldier and statesman. He spent most of his time in Europe but was nevertheless a true patriot. He considered himself Venezuelan, not Spanish.

During a visit to London, Miranda was approached by the British Government, which offered to finance a revolt in Venezuela. At the moment England, troubled by Napoleon and the defunct Spanish monarchy, could wish nothing better than revolution in Latin America. Miranda accepted the offer eagerly.

The first attempt, made in 1806, was a fiasco, and Miranda fled for his life. His exile lasted only four years. By 1810 other Creoles in Venezuela were organizing revolt, and Miranda came home to lead them. There were successes at first, but unfortunately, because of a misunderstanding, his officers thought he had betrayed them. Included in these was Simón Bolívar, the Venezuelan who ultimately became the towering genius in the story of South American liberation from Spain. Miranda was turned over to the Royalists, was sent to Spain and died in a dungeon in Cadiz in 1816. Bolívar carried on the work. The reputation of this great man is legendary. He and his triumphs have assumed almost mythical proportions.

Simón Bolívar was born in Caracas, Venezuela, in 1783, the son of a wealthy planter. From earliest childhood his thinking and his actions were flamboyant, romantic, independent. While still very young, he was sent to Europe for schooling and there fell under the influence of Simon Rodriguez, his tutor. Rodriguez was a learned disciple of Jacques Rousseau and others of the great 18th-century school of European thought. He was precisely the man to make a lasting impression on the high-spirited and intelligent young Creole from Venezuela. Together the two of them toured Europe on foot—studying philosophy, reading, talking.

In addition to the association with Rodriguez, one other incident is said to have influenced Bolívar more than anything else in his life. This was the coronation of Napoleon as Emperor of France in 1804. As he watched the fireworks bursting in the skies over Fontainebleau, he wept openly at this tragic betrayal of the hopes of the French Revolution and was at the same time exulted at the obvious results of what a powerful individual could do when driven by dreams of glory. This double side to Bolívar's character was to give him his greatness—and his tragedy. In later years, when offered the opportunity to become a king by his grateful countrymen, he steadfastly refused even though a part of him cried out for the honor. His belief in freedom and in the right of men to govern themselves won over personal ambition.

Bolívar returned from Europe to take part in the ill-fated attempt of Miranda in 1812. From this time on, the struggle was joined. The battles and the campaigns raged over the entire northern part of South America. The plains, the jungles, the icy peaks of the Andes, all were areas in which Bolívar and his armies—at times reduced to a ragged handful of men—struggled for liberty.

Far to the south, in the colony of La Plata (now Argentina), the fight also was taking shape. Here, the effort was at first directed against—of all nations—Great Britain. Always with an eye cocked to the long view of the future, always practical and, above all, hypersensitive to world trade and shifting balances of power, England sent expeditionary forces in 1807 and again in 1810 to try and occupy Buenos Aires. It is indeed high tribute to the might of Britain in those days that while joined in a death struggle with Napoleon and faced with problems in Canada with the United States, she could still muster men and ships to send to distant Argentina.

The Creole militia in Argentina had no use for Spain, but even less for England. They repulsed the British and, in the absence of any government or direction from Madrid, and still loyal to Spain, they set up committees to rule in the King's name. The desire for real freedom ran deep, however, and before long it exploded. Creoles fought with Spaniards, Republicans fought with Royalists, Liberals with Conservatives. In spite of the dissension, the committees managed to hold the huge province under control; but eventually the edges of this control began to crumble. Independent revolutionary governments were established, although precariously, in what are now Uruguay, Paraguay and Argentina.

Across the great Andes, along the Pacific Coast, the same pattern of rebellion was taking place in the areas that eventually came to be Chile, Peru and Ecuador. The great leader of this movement was a Chilean Creole of Irish ancestry named Bernardo O'Higgins. O'Higgins was defeated by Spanish loyalist troops, but the defeat was due more to disagreement among the revolutionaries than to military action.

In 1816 the scene in the south was set for the final act. The chief character was a Creole—José de San Martín. San Martín had been born in the northern part of La Plata and elected a career in the Spanish Army. In Europe he became one of the few Creoles to achieve high rank. After serving for 22 years in some of the hardest fighting, he returned home to the land of his birth after the downfall of Napoleon.

San Martín was a tough, experienced fighting man. He was also an avid monarchist. He had fought for years for the crown of Spain, and he believed in it. More important, though, was the fact of his birth. He was a Creole, an Argentinian. His dream for a free Argentina was stronger than all his devotion to Spain.

He wasted no time and plunged headlong into the struggle. He conceived an audacious plan to cross the Andes, fight his way northward and ultimately free the rich heartland of Spanish power—golden Peru itself. San Martín was a patriot, but he was no impractical dreamer. He was a skilled professional soldier to the tips of his toes, not the man to embark upon such a plan without preparation. He had no intention of going off half-cocked, settling down instead to a long period of collecting supplies and training men. Three years were to go by while San Martín bided his time and laboriously made preparations. The southern part of the continent stewed in its own juices. Other, more impetuous men fought a hundred useless battles; San Martín could not be tempted to strike until all was ready.

In the north, Simón Bolívar kept the flame alight, at times with complete lack of hope, forlornly losing battle after battle. While all this was going on, while the people seethed with restlessness, without direction or real preparation, another event took place. It was to alter the entire course of the struggle for independence. At first the effect was disastrous.

This event was the defeat of Napoleon at Waterloo in 1815. The end of the Napoleonic Wars released tens upon tens of thousands of tough, experienced fighting men who were completely loyal to the crown of Spain, now restored to power. The Spanish Government wasted no time, money or energy in sending these troops to the New World to make one last, gigantic effort to force her erring children back into line.

These soldiers and their veteran generals had learned their trade the hard way—fighting the French over half of Europe. The struggling South American revolutionaries found themselves with far more on their hands than they could handle. Starry-eyed and emotional patriotic amateur soldiers were no match for the hard-bitten professionals who descended upon them.

Well-equipped and confident, these newly arrived Spanish soldiers won victory after victory. The rebellions and revolutions which had flared with their small successes all over Latin America were squelched. The weak, quarreling little republics that had been set up fell like overripe plums to the rampaging troops. The only country which was not wholly reconquered was Argentina. Ironically, it held out because of aid it received from the nation which had tried to subdue it just a few years previously—England. In complete defiance of Spain, her recent ally, England sent very real help to the Creoles in Argentina.

Old dogs are supposed not to be able to learn new tricks. So, apparently, are old restored kings unable to learn anything new. No sooner had the colonial empire been returned to the fold than King Ferdinand put back into effect all the old, hated edicts, harsher than ever. Even those subjects who had remained loyal to the crown during the years of turmoil were appalled. An enlightened policy in the colonies might very well have preserved the empire intact. As it was, the fires of freedom burned all the more brightly. Though the odds were worse than ever before, the struggle continued. More and more of the masses of Creoles became willing to do anything to get the ancient, crushing weight of cruel Spain from their backs. Added to this was the fact that Latin America had had a small taste of freedom and found it good. So, almost without interruption and in the face of increasing resistance, battle after battle lost, the struggle continued.

There were two very small pockets of hope. In the south, in still-free Argentina, José de San Martín laboriously tried to make soldiers out of farmers, city men, miners and ranchers. In the north, the work was pitifully slow. Simón Bolívar, his "forces" shattered, fled for his life to the island of Jamaica.

6

AFTER CATCHING HIS BREATH on British Jamaica, Bolívar issued a famous proclamation, known as the "Jamaica Letter." Although there seemed no cause for optimism, Bolívar expressed hopes for victory and pledged himself to continue the struggle.

Back in South America, for two years Bolívar led the life of a fugitive. With ragged guerrillas he fought skirmish after skirmish with the enemy, most of the time only a fast jump ahead of Spanish troops. Eventually he earned what San Martín far to the south already knew. Independence was never to be won fighting small-hit-and-run battles against tough regulars. Accordingly, he established a headquarters deep in the mountains and jungles in the upper reaches of the great Orinoco River and spent two full years assembling and trying to equip an army.

The desperate Creole population went all out to help. Men volunteered to fight. Land was sold to raise money. Loans were obtained. Jewels, heirlooms and other precious family relics were turned into cash. In a thousand and one ways funds were collected to buy artillery, muskets, ammunition, horses and all the other supplies needed to wage war. Even a few foreign mercenaries were recruited. At one time Bolívar had with him a battalion of tough Irishmen hired on the streets of Dublin.

By 1817 Bolívar was ready for an all-out effort. Because of the preparation and also because of the increased corruption and inefficiency of the Spanish, slowly the tide began turning. Although many desperate years of hard fighting lay ahead, people began to take hope.

The freedom fighters were also fortunate when they were joined by several thousand horsemen from the Orinoco plains cattle country. These hard-riding cavalrymen were led by José Antonio Paez, a legendary bull of an outdoor man who had spent more life in the saddle than afoot. Paez was hard, cruel and unbelievably merciless to prisoners. He and Bolívar clashed many times because of this. By now also, thousands of Creole veterans had been released from the Spanish Armies in Europe, and many of these experienced soldiers returned home to take up arms for freedom.

Bolívar was convinced that the concentration of Spanish troops in Venezuela was too strong for his army, so, like San Martín in the south, he crossed the Andes. After making its way through the lowland jungles and then scaling the incredible, icy peaks of the mountains, the army descended upon the astonished Spanish garrisons in New Granada, or what is today known as Colombia. Bogotá fell to the revolutionaries in 1818.

Retracing his steps, Bolívar led his men back to Venezuela, where he defeated the Royalists in 1821. Once again turning westward, they crossed the Andes for the *second time* and joined the second-in-command, José Antonio de Sucre, in Ecuador. Together they routed the Spanish in a bloody battle fought near Quito.

Meanwhile, San Martín had fought his way through the endless "altiplano," or highland plains of the southern Andes, and was working his way up the western coast of the continent toward Peru. Helped by Bernardo O'Higgins, San Martín liberated Chile in 1818.

Only Peru in all of South America remained Spanish, and San Martín was convinced that liberation was not possible as long as Peru held out. He wrote, "The war will not be over until we are in Lima." Accordingly, he assembled a fleet of transports and put it under the command of Lord Thomas Cochrane, an English sailor of fortune. Cochrane knew his business. Sailing up the coast, he safely landed 6,000 of San Martín's soldiers in Peru. They captured Lima in 1821. But apparently the staunch Peruvian royalists were not at all eager for independence. In the countryside they reorganized and fought San Martín to a standstill. He finally turned northward again to seek help from Bolívar who was still mopping up after the campaigns in Ecuador.

The two liberators met in Guayaquil in 1822 in several private conferences but were unable to reach any satisfactory decisions about future plans. Exactly what was discussed between San Martin and Bolívar is one of history's best-kept secrets, which neither ever divulged.

Educated guesses about these conversations say that San Martín probably offered to serve under Bolívar during the battles for the final conquest of Peru. They also say that San Martín insisted that only under a strong monarchy would the nations that were to be created have any chance for lasting stability. Bolívar is said to have turned down both these ideas.

The speculation is interesting and is possibly correct because of the personalities of the two men. They both hated the Spanish bitterly, but San Martín was an avid believer in a strong, royalist type of government while Bolívar believed only in democracy. He would listen to no talk of monarchies; he would tolerate no suggestions for a return to rule by kings in South America.

Immediately after the meetings, San Martín sent Bolívar a present of a horse and a brace of pistols and with no more delay set out for home in Buenos Aires. Feeling that his work was done, he shortly sailed for Europe, never to return to his homeland. He died abroad, self-exiled.

Bolívar's work was far from finished. In a series of extremely bitter and bloody battles, he and Sucre finally defeated the holdouts in Peru—the last bastion of Spanish power. South America was free.

In spite of Bolívar's pleas for unity, Lower Peru separated from Upper Peru to form an independent nation. It gave itself the name of Bolivia, after the liberator. Bolívar himself wrote its first constitution, and Sucre was elected its first President.

As with the disillusioned San Martín, Bolívar's last years were bitter and unhappy. His dream had been for South America to divide itself into several large federations. Each was to have been composed of a number of smaller states and each patterned somewhat along the order of the United States of America.

This was never to be. Only the magic of his presence kept the federations from disintegrating as fast as he set them up. The moment he left, ambitious, quarreling men took over; only when Bolívar returned was order restored. Again and again Bolívar's loyal followers begged him to set up governments which the politically uneducated Creoles would understand and respect—anything with authority and power, even a monarchy if necessary. Bolívar steadfastly refused, although in his heart he no doubt knew this was the only way. To the end he refused to be elected a king or an emperor or to take part in any way in the establishment of such a system.

Like Napoleon, Bolívar was filled with dreams of greatness and with lust for personal power and glory. At the same time, he was stopped from yielding to them by his deep belief in democracy. He refused to abandon his ideals either for self-glorification or even for what at the moment seemed to be for the good of the people. He would not compromise. There was never a coronation or any fireworks for him.

Bolívar struggled on to bring peace to the people of South America. As fast as he put out the fires of discontent in one place they flared up in another. Finally, utterly worn out from fifteen years of terrible fighting—twelve of which were literally spent in the saddle—and dying of tuberculosis, Bolívar determined to go into exile abroad, as San Martín had done.

On his way to take ship for Europe, Simón Bolívar died in the hot little tropical port of Santa Marta, on the coast of Colombia. With him were only two or three of his old comrades. The others had all drifted away, to feather their own nests, it is said, in one way or another.

Among the great men that the Western Hemisphere has produced, Simón Bolívar ranks high. He was earthy, practical, romantic, aristocratic, intelligent—a dictionary of contradictions. He was also a stubborn, bull-headed man who could not be swayed by those close to him who were perhaps more clear-eyed than he about the political abilities of their fellow-South Americans. He believed in democracy and died believing in it.

Bolívar's deeds and his sayings are legendary. Two perhaps are worth repeating.

As he lay dying in Santa Marta, gasping for breath in the hot humid air, he stated bitterly, "Those who have served the revolution have ploughed the sea." He must have had premonitions.

Bolívar was a close friend and great admirer of Benjamin Franklin, and one of his prized possessions was a lock of Franklin's hair, which he carried with him always in a locket about his neck. As he neared death, this locket seemed to be the one object which represented truth and steadfastness. Only this keepsake seemed to have meaning, and he died with the locket in his hand.

After Bolívar's death, the dire predictions of his comrades came true. All the federations fell apart into many small independent nations, each fiercely jealous of its status and quarrelsome with its neighbors and ruled by a succession of strong-men "leaders."

This was probably for two reasons. The masses of the people were in no sense prepared for responsible self-government. Long, long centuries of ruthless rule and exploitation by Spain had planted no democratic seeds. They were accustomed to governments run by tight, powerful groups with a leader at the head. They felt comfortable with someone strong in charge. If matters were mismanaged or abused, or if democracy was lost in the shuffle, at least affairs were run somehow, and not abandoned to futile talk, quarreling and chaos.

The other reason had nothing to do with the people. It was a matter of geography. The vast swamps and jungles and the impassable mountains were such overwhelming barriers to transportation and communication that cohesion into large political groups was nearly impossible.

International recognition of the independence of the new Latin-American states came at different times. Great Britain and the United States accorded them the dignity while gunfire still echoed across the mountains. Spain was somewhat slower! She recognized the last, Honduras, in 1895. Cuba and Puerto Rico remained Spanish colonies until 1899.

All during the long and confused struggle in South America, Northern Americans and the American Government were most sympathetic. It was a struggle they could understand, and their best wishes were with their neighbors to the south.

Never a man to miss larger issues or long-term implications, Thomas Jefferson wrote, ". . . in whatever kind of governments they will end, they will be American governments, no longer involved in the never-ceasing broils of Europe. The European nations constitute a separate division of the globe; their localities make them part of a distinct system; they have a set of interests of their own in which it is our business never to engage ourselves. America has a hemisphere to itself. It must have its separate system of interests which must not be subordinated to those of Europe. The insulated state in which nature has placed the American continents should so far avail that no spark of war kindled in the other quarters of the globe should be wafted across the wide oceans which separate us from them, and it will be so."

There was no doubt either as to the interest of the ordinary American people in the struggle for freedom in Latin America. Americans *believed* in freedom—their own or anyone else's. They did not like to see their nextdoor neighbors subject to a despotic king, and their best sympathies went out to them.

These feelings were practical, emotional and romantic. They were well expressed by Henry Clay. He spoke in the House of Representatives in 1818, long before freedom was a fact in Latin America. He said, "We are their great example. Of us they continually speak as brothers having a similar origin. . . . In many instances they employ the very language and sentiments of our own revolutionary papers. But it is sometimes said that they are too ignorant and too superstitious to admit of the existence of free government. . . . I deny the alleged fact of ignorance . . . that they lack the capacity for free government . . . and that we are to be indifferent to their fate. It is the doctrine of thrones that man is too ignorant to govern himself, to be trampled upon by kings. . . . Once independent, whatever the form of the governments established, these governments will be animated by an American feeling. Highly important is the consideration of the nature of their governments. That is a question, however, for themselves. We have no right to prescribe for them. They are and ought to be the sole judges for themselves. I am strongly inclined to believe that they will in most, if not in all parts, of their countries establish free governments."

As country after country won and proclaimed its freedom, the deep differences between the Old and the New Worlds grew greater and more obvious. In spite of the fervent hopes and predictions of Jefferson, Clay, Monroe and countless others in both North and South America, Europe was not yet done with the New World. Events now took a turn which sent the United States flying down the path to even greater isolationism and which made it necessary for President Monroe to make a definite public stand spelling it out.

American public opinion was ready for the statement. The twist that world affairs now took provided the circumstances which made it necessary.

7

IN THE WAKE of the wreckage left by Napoleon in Europe, the underhanded power plays of the restored monarchies reached new heights. And, worse, every single dark plan for the extension of power or for the preservation of aristocratic political systems which was hatched seemed to wing across the Atlantic and find a perch in the White House or the halls of Congress. The direction that history took as Europe picked itself up from the tragedy of the Napoleonic Wars raised spectres that chilled American hearts.

First appearances were innocent. A quarter of a century of bloodletting was over, and America, with the rest of the world, rejoiced. The Congress of Vienna, the meetings at which the peace terms were worked out, must have been a gorgeous spectacle. The dazzling pageantry of royalty was on display. There were kings, queens, emperors and empresses in abundance. There were dashing military men, dripping with medals, lace and gold braid. Elegant diplomats competed with handsome courtiers for the favors of powdered and bejeweled ladies. And of course, there was the vast retinue of servants and flunkeys needed to support the show. Between sessions of serious negotiations, opportunities were plentiful for the magnificent assemblage to make merry in the countryside, at fetes and at gorgeous balls.

Americans may have snickered at the glitter, but there was nothing alarming in it, nor in the terms of the peace treaty which were set up to prevent any recurrence of the war. It was reasonable that England, Russia, Austria and Prussia join to form the Quadruple Alliance for the purpose of discouraging France from breaking loose again. It was likewise sensible that these "big four" provide for regular meetings to examine the political situation of Europe and to take such steps as might be necessary to maintain peace and prosperity.

And so America observed the goings-on in Vienna and applauded what seemed to be genuine efforts to establish lasting peace. Americans hoped for the best but at the same time thanked their lucky stars they were removed from all of it.

There were, however, plenty of cynics on both sides of the Atlantic. They hinted openly that the real purpose of the Vienna Congress was not so much to preserve peace as it was to preserve royalty. They stated flatly that the true aim of the Quadruple Alliance at the gorgeous banquet in Vienna was to carve and serve up the fat melon of Napoleon's once mighty empire.

Among all the regal participants at the Congress, one, however, was an idealist of purest hue. This was Tsar Alexander of Russia. He felt that his role in the deliberations should be an important one and that his advice would be heeded by a continent sick to death of war. He believed that he could speak with authority. He had laid the groundwork for Napoleon's final defeat by having the courage to set fire to his capital city of Moscow and to order his troops to harass the retreating French as they struggled back across the icy plains to France. The Russians also had played a very important part in later battles which led to Waterloo.

For years Alexander had nursed a plan which he was sure would guarantee eternal peace in Europe. So sure was he that he could dominate the Congress, he dispensed with the services of his Foreign Minister, Count Tolstoy. He should have been more practical. The Tsar and his idealism were politely but most effectively ignored by such wily professional statesmen as Castlereagh of England, Talleyrand of France and Metternich of Austria.

As these smooth gentlemen gleefully divided Napoleon's real estate, Alexander had to sit on the sidelines. For services rendered, the principal chefs were pleased to carve off a nice slice of Poland and serve it up to him. However, Alexander was determined about his plan. He called another conference on his own, inviting such august personages as the Emperor of Austria and the King of Prussia. He put on a tremendous show for the guests. The ground shook as Cossack cavalry, grenadiers and artillery wheeled and marched. For a finale there was a giant outdoor religious ceremony at which the Orthodox service of Mass was conducted with regal pomp.

After the preliminaries, Alexander revealed his plan. It was to ensure peace by adhering to religious principles rather than to faith in soldiery. The prospective signers were invited to put their names to a document which manifested "before the whole universe their unshakeable determination to take as their sole guide, both in the administration of their respective states and in their political relations with other governments, the precepts of religion, namely, the rules of Justice, Christian charity and peace."

This document was unlike any the diplomats had ever seen. Instead of spelling matters out in detail and setting up rules to be enforced by military strength, they were merely asked to promise to be "good." They would accomplish this by observing "the duties which the Divine Saviour had taught to mankind." They were to remain united by "the bonds of true and indissoluble fraternity" as laid down in the Holy Scriptures and to "extend a fatherly care and protection to their subjects" and to consider themselves "members of one and the same Christian nation . . . and confess that this Christian world . . . had no other sovereign than Him to Whom alone rightful power belongs."

The short pact invited all who professed to these sacred principles to enter with "ardor and affection into this Holy Alliance." The pact came to be known as the Holy Alliance.

Austria and Prussia were the principal participants at this remarkable meeting. They signed the treaty with a certain reluctance, but nevertheless with goodwill. While the wording and the aims seemed vague, it cost them nothing and they were not promising anybody anything. They said only that they would behave themselves—whatever this might mean. Eventually, every monarch in Europe—with three exceptions—signed the pact.

George IV of England politely declined. The document was a personal agreement between absolute monarchs, and he, alas, was no longer absolute. He had a Parliament to consider. The Pope also passed, explaining that he could not enter into a religious treaty which included heretics—in this case Protestants. The Sultan of Turkey also was left out. After all, he wasn't even a Christian, so what could he possibly know of such lofty matters?

Oddly enough, the United States of America was invited to join the group of royal persons. After serious consultation with President Monroe, the Secretary of State, John Adams, forwarded instructions to the American Minister in St. Petersburg. Adams was quite stuffy about the whole matter, reiterating in strong language the growing policy of American isolationism and the country's determination to stay aloof from European problems. It was all too complicated for America and seemed precisely the kind of foreign entanglement the nation wished most to avoid. In the last sentence of his note, Adams said that "this consideration alone would be decisive for declining participation in that league, which is the President's absolute and irrevocable determination, although he trusts that no occasion will present itself rendering it necessary to make that determination known by explicit refusal."

In other words, America was going to stay out, but hoped it could be polite about the whole matter. The Minister to the court of the Tsar had to walk a very tight and narrow path. He must never allow the occasion to arise where he would be obliged to give out a blunt "no."

Before much time passed, America was to be more than grateful it was not involved in the Holy Alliance. As matters progressed it became known to the people of the United States, and to a good many others in the world at large, as the extremely Unholy Alliance. To the democratic, liberal peoples of the earth, the Alliance was the arch-enemy of progress. It was the vicious instrument of reaction, the open enemy of freedom. Far more than the traditional political-military Quadruple Alliance, the mystical, semireligious Holy Alliance became a dark and dangerous specter which haunted Americans and all others who professed a belief in the rights of man.

The principles of the Monroe Doctrine for many years had been alive in the hearts of Americans. The time was coming closer when they were to be fired bluntly, like a broadside, at the whole world. The activities of the Holy Alliance loaded and cocked the guns.

The diplomats and the royal political connivers who sought to mold and rule the world after Napoleon's downfall found just the weapon they needed in Tsar Alexander's pact. The vague idealism, the appeal to religion, the reliance upon conscience and "divinely inspired" concepts, could be stretched to cover just about anything. The statesmen took full advantage of this.

The wiliest architect of the new Europe trying to rise up out of the ruins of twenty-five years of suffering was an Austrian. His name was just as imposing as his reputation. He was Prince Clemens Wenzel Nepomuk Lothar von Metternich. For all practical purposes, he was the chief statesman of the Holy Alliance. Skillfully he practiced his trade. He checked and counterchecked, planned and counterplanned, balanced and counterbalanced, throughout the courts from one end of Europe to the other.

Metternich's methods were reaction, brutality, force and opposition to any democratic process. Europe was honeycombed with spies—professional agitators who could stir up any kind of trouble that might be needed to make intervention, either military or political, excusable. Metternich depended upon dark intrigue, poison, censorship, ruthless suppression of thought, kidnappings. He recognized that a free press was one of the great foes of reaction, and so newspapers everywhere were closed or destroyed. "Order" was kept by force—anywhere, anytime, for any reason. The aim was to preserve things as they were or, better yet, to restore them as they had been. Go back, never forward. Metternich's voice was that of total conservatism at its worst, and his name became anathema to believers in democracy.

Eventually all the monarchies of Europe embraced and enforced this new and potent weapon against progress. In the name of the Holy Alliance, Austria suppressed a movement for freedom in Italy. France interfered in Spain. Even that idealist, Tsar Alexander, stuck a finger in the broth. He aided the Turkish Sultan, who was a Moslem, in brutally suppressing a rebellion for liberty by Greek Christians. All of Europe happily and busily united in enforcing the aims of the Holy Alliance as interpreted by Metternich.

America looked on with horror. Morally Americans condemned the proceedings, but, more than this, they were filled with grim forebodings. There was nothing at the moment which seemed to threaten the United States, but international politics were as complicated then as they are now. No matter how fervently Americans wished to be let alone, they knew in their hearts it was only partly up to them. No one could tell for certain what direction the floods of ambition in Europe might take, or in what grim way the New World could become involved.

In 1818 the country was treated to an inkling of what could happen. That year the Holy Alliance held its meetings at Aix-la-Chapelle, in France. The overtones were ominous when delegates brought up the possibility of the Alliance poking its nose into the boiling affairs of Spain's Latin-American troubles. Nothing was decided upon, but even the mention of the subject had been enough to cause shudders in the White House.

America's position at the moment was especially complicated. The government was about to enter into negotiations with Spain for the purchase of the Florida Territory. Sympathy was all for the struggling South Americans, whose independence was still very much in the balance; but if America gave encouragement to the revolutionaries, how would the Holy Alliance react? And what would happen to the dealings with Spain for Florida?

President Monroe and his advisers proceeded with caution. First things had to come first, and the acquisition of Florida was high on the list. The treaty by which they took over the territory was signed in February of 1821. Just two months later, Henry Clay pushed a resolution through the House of Representatives expressing America's readiness to recognize the infant nations of South America as they became independent.

America was moving fast and dangerously, but there was no alternative as Europe also moved into high gear. When Congress expressed willingness to recognize the new independent states, it was fully aware of the slap it was giving the Holy Alliance. No one kept the country in doubt for long as to possible developments.

Out of the pious and divinely hopeful idealism of Tsar Alexander had evolved the concept that the most sacred duty of the Holy Alliance was to uphold the divine rights of kings, and to protect their positions. King Ferdinand VII of Spain was an ineffectual monarch. Even in the eyes of his fellow kings of the Holy Alliance he was of little account—except in one important respect. He was "legitimate." His blood line was purest royal blue, and his "right" to the throne of Spain was beyond question.

Ferdinand was so useless and incompetent, however, that even the most loyal of his own subjects became fed up. They deposed him and threw him in jail. The members of the Holy Alliance, particularly France, had had a terrible lesson in the French Revolution. They knew full well just where rebellion against kings could lead and consequently took very much to heart the actions of the Spanish against Ferdinand.

A powerfully rearmed France marched into Spain and once more restored poor Ferdinand to his throne. But even the Holy Alliance came to the conclusion that something would have to be done about him and his continuing troubles in Latin America.

At the next Holy Alliance Congress, held in Verona, Italy, in 1822, the question America had been dreading was brought into the open. No words were minced. The question was whether or not the powers of the Alliance should take immediate and forceful action to settle once and for all the problem of Spain's nearly defunct Latin-American empire. Time was running out. If Latin America was going to be preserved for Ferdinand as a part of imperial Europe's colonial system, with perhaps goodly slices hacked off for other Alliance powers, then they'd have to move fast.

In Washington, lights burned late in the White House. In Cabinet meetings the subject was hashed and rehashed and examined from every possible angle. Who was bluffing whom? Or was anybody just bluffing? This might very well be for real. There was no way of knowing for sure.

Lights burned late also in the Foreign Ministries of European governments, and with good cause. The decisions to be taken at Verona and the subsequent actions which might be sanctioned could affect powerful Old World nations as profoundly as they could America. France, Spain, Portugal, Austria, Russia, Prussia, England—all of them breathed warily and gazed from Verona across the Atlantic to the Americas with deep speculation. The stakes were enormous. The penalties for a false move were almost beyond calculation.

In particular, the men guiding the destinies of two of these European giants pondered deeply. These two powers were Russia and England.

8

DENMARK, 1681. The little Danish boy who was born that year was no different from many of his countrymen in that he grew up to be a sailor. Yet this youngster was different from the others in one important way. He was not content to roam the world in peaceful merchant ships. He wanted to be an explorer. The time was to come when he would be known as one of the toughest, most ruthless and most resourceful men ever to gaze over the horizons of unknown seas to fresh and distant lands.

His name was Vitus Jonassen Bering. He joined the Russian Navy and eventually was sent by Catherine the Great to conduct explorations in the Pacific. Bering died, shipwrecked, on a bleak and icy island off the coast of Siberia, but not before he had established once and for all the geography of the North Pacific. The narrow passage between Siberia and Alaska still bears his name—Bering Strait.

Upon Bering's discoveries rested all of Russia's claims to territory on the continent of North America. These claims were not modest, and by 1823 they caused much furrowing of brows and concern among President Monroe and his Cabinet.

When Bering died on the rocky and wind-swept island, the scurvy-ridden remnants of his crew hammered together a small boat out of the timbers of their wrecked ship. In it they sailed back to Siberia and eventually made their way on foot across the steppes and forests to Russia proper. They brought with them news of a most wonderful discovery, news of an overflowing treasure chest for all those hardy enough to go after it.

This bonanza was fur. The forests and the seas along the northwestern coasts of the continent were swarming with fur-bearing animals of every description. The most valuable of the lot was a small marine animal called a sea otter. Sea otter pelts were heavy with a warm, silky fur the likes of which the world had never seen before. Otters were gentle, unsuspecting creatures, easy to kill. The waters swarmed with them.

Russian traders introduced the fur to China, and it was an instant success. Hundreds of thousands of the little sea otters were slaughtered to make warm, elegant clothing for the Chinese aristocracy.

Ships of other nations could not let such a bonanza pass, and they too began carrying sea-otter pelts to the Orient. New England traders and shipmasters were particularly active. Out of this trade developed the famous three-way commerce from America's east coast, and many a staid Boston fortune was founded on it.

Ships left home with whale oil, glassware, lamps, nails, shoes, tools and other manufactured goods, which were sold, quite illegally, to the neglected Spanish colonies in California. When the holds were empty, the crews were turned to killing sea otters. The pelts were taken to China and sold for fantastic sums, which in turn were used to fill the ships with silks, satins, spices, ivory, tea and other products of the Orient, which would command enormous prices back in New England. Thus a vessel, in one single voyage, although a very long and hazardous one, could load and unload three times.

Trouble arose almost at once. The Russians did not take kindly to this invasion of their territory, particularly by the American ships, the most numerous and audacious of the poachers. Officially and unofficially the Russians did everything to stop it.

Through a private but government-sponsored corporation known as the Russian-American Trading Company, Russian settlements, trading posts and influence spread southward. By 1800 there were thriving Russian fur towns at Kodiak and Sitka. Taking a still further step, Tsar Alexander granted the company exclusive rights in all territories above latitude 55 degrees north, a line cutting across the middle of what is now Canada. He gave his subjects permission to establish settlements as far as they liked on either side of that line as long as they stayed out of the property which obviously belonging to other nations. In line with this, by 1812 the Russian-American Trading Company had established a prosperous settlement—Fort Rossiya, now known as Fort Ross—a mere eighty miles north of the Spanish village of San Francisco!

Since, under the old monarchial rule, Spain's colonies were forbidden the right to trade with any nation other than Spain, these California outposts were always in a state of hardship. Spanish ships to such distant outposts were few and far between. When the empire finally was overthrown and the colonies became independent states, California became a province—Alta California—of Mexico. The first governor under the Republic of Mexico's flag was a native San Franciscan, a Creole named Luís Antonio Arguello. He immediately relaxed the old restrictions against foreign trade, and one of his first acts was to grant the Russian-American Trading Company permission to establish more trading posts in California. He also gave them the right to hunt sea otters on a share basis, anywhere they liked along California's lengthy coast.

Until then the Russians and their aspirations on the Pacific coast had been regarded with a certain, but vague, apprehension in Washington. There had been conversations in which diplomats felt each other out and gingerly talked around the edges of the problem, but nothing had ever come of them. In a way the Pacific coast seemed as remote as the moon. The Russians in Alaska and the Spanish in California really didn't have too much bearing on the immediate national life of the United States, especially since Americans and their government had been occupied with other pressing matters during these early years.

In 1823, however, the country had time to draw a deep breath and consider some of the long-range implications of current problems. No one really knew what the future held, but the feeling was growing that the distant Pacific shores of the continent were sooner or later going to be a real part of that future. Still, the concern was mild until a new development changed it overnight to real alarm.

As with so many things in those days, the shape of the world seemed subject to the schemes of the Holy Alliance, and the Pacific was not exempt. Tsar Alexander hadn't been doing too well with Alliance grabs in Europe, so the time seemed ripe to him for a modest little acquisition in his own back yard. He issued an official proclamation, or *ukase,* as it was called in Tsarist Russia, which left no doubt as to his intentions. Alexander granted exclusive commercial rights to the Russian-American Trading Company clear down to 51 degrees north latitude and prohibited *all* foreign vessels from coming within one hundred "Italian miles" of the coast.

There were teeth in this decree. All ships which violated it were subject to immediate confiscation. Alexander's reshuffling of geography now claimed, as an exclusive starter, all the seas and land lying just a shade to the north of what is now the boundary between the United States and Canada.

The Tsar may have thought of this remote wilderness land as being up for grabs and simply moved in before anyone else staked out a claim. He also might have done what he did as a feeler, to see if anyone would object. If he had any illusions at all, they were quickly blasted. Great Britain and the United States, particularly the latter, did object, and in no uncertain terms. Alexander had paced off quite a piece of real estate, and America did not hesitate to let him know its feelings.

The Monroe Doctrine was proclaimed on December 2nd, 1823, but now, six months before, it was given semipublic expression for the first time by the Secretary of State, John Quincy Adams. The words were his, but they nevertheless stated so fundamental a policy that they surely were uttered with Monroe's full approval.

John Quincy Adams was the son of the second President, John Adams. He himself was elected President following Monroe and gave his father, who was still living, the honor of being the only Chief Executive to see his son also elected to the office.

John Quincy Adams was a proud and independent man. He often defended, quite alone, those things which he believed to be right. He was aggressive, pugnacious and acid-tongued but also highly intelligent and of unquestioned integrity. Adams was a strong isolationist and made no bones about it. For example, in 1819 he was negotiating with Spain for the purchase of Florida. In the agreement he insisted that Spain renounce *all* rights—east and west—

north of 42 degrees latitude, the line which ultimately became the southern boundaries of Oregon and Idaho. In a Cabinet meeting Adams stated that the world "must be familiarized with the idea of considering our proper dominion to be the continent of North America."

United States and Great Britain jointly administered this vast and remote wilderness to some northern point yet to be established. The whole territory, known simply as the Columbia River Region, became the subject of a hot debate with the British Minister, Stratford Canning, in 1821. Adams forcefully defended his position and in so doing took a further step along the route that was finally clarified in the Monroe Doctrine.

In the talk, Adams said, "We certainly did suppose that the British Government had come to the conclusion that there would be neither policy nor profit in cavilling with us about this territory on the North American continent."

Replied Canning, "And in this you include our northern provinces on the continent?"

"No," said Adams. "There the boundary is marked, and we have no disposition to encroach upon it. Keep what is yours, but leave the rest of the continent to us."

The whole matter of colonization and empires was hateful to Adams' proud and independent democratic spirit. By 1822 he was ready to go even farther on the subject. He said, "The whole system of modern colonization is an abuse of government, and it is time that it should come to an end."

Such a declaration was more a political theory than hard and actual practice; but even so, Adams' feelings were rooted in the tough, everyday world of economics. By its nature the colonial system was commercial monopoly. Colonies traded mainly with their mother country, and goods were shipped back and forth in vessels flying that country's flag. At this time American foreign trade and shipping were of enormous importance to the nation. To live, America had to trade and ship in freedom, where and how she could. Thus Adams was not merely theorizing when he attacked the colonial system. He was defending that which was vital to America.

When Tsar Alexander issued his decree extending Russia's interests to 51 degrees and prohibiting ships of other nations even to approach the shores of the territory, Adams was ready. Boldly he took the bull by the horns and challenged the Tsar. Russian ambitions gave him the opportunity to express his and the government's feelings regarding any further colonization on the North American continent.

In the summer of 1823, about five months before the Monroe Doctrine was proclaimed, Adams summoned Baron Tuyll, the Russian Minister to the United States. Although Tsar Alexander had by now indicated a willingness to negotiate, Adams spelled it out to Tuyll. He told him flatly that "we would contest the right of Russia to any territorial establishment on this continent, and that we should assume distinctly the principle that the American continents are no longer subject to any new European colonization."

Five days later, in an informal letter accompanying instructions to the American Minister in Russia, Adams was even more explicit. He wrote, "There can, perhaps, be no better time for saying, frankly and explicitly, to the Russian Government, that the future peace of the world, and the interests of Russia herself, cannot be promoted by Russian settlements upon any part of the American continent. With the exception of the British establishments north of the United States, the remainder of both the American continents must henceforth be left to the management of American hands."

This was strong language. The America of 1823 was a small mite beside the giant of Russia. It is doubtful that Adams intended to convey to Russia that she must abandon her long-established bases in Alaska. He surely could not have believed that the United States could back up such a demand. What is more likely is that Adams was expressing a political point of view for guidance in the future for any other country which might throw greedy glances in this direction.

Whether or not Adams had any right to make such statements, based on logic or on previous treaties, is still debated. Alaska, Canada and the whole Northwest Territory was enormous, raw, unexplored. Boundaries and areas of influence were mostly imaginary. Theoretically this gigantic, empty portion of the earth's surface should have been open to colonization by anyone.

Practically, though, Adams and President Monroe were looking far into the future. In using language so strong they were running a tremendous bluff and were outlining how they hoped things would be in the future, not sticking to the facts as they were. The words stated America's position, and it was important that the rest of the world know exactly what that position was.

Also, Russia had been stopped, although nobody knew it at the time. Alexander and his Holy Alliance had something new to think about before Russia sent any more expeditions into the Pacific and southward along California. The whole matter was settled much later by diplomacy. Russian boundaries were put at 54 degrees north, and Americans were conceded trading privileges far above this line.

Out of this diplomatic flurry with Russia developed the noncolonization portions of the Monroe Doctrine. It is very important to remember that when the Doctrine was finally proclaimed, there was no way for Adams or Monroe to know what the Tsar had in mind. The affair with Russia in the Northwest had not yet been settled, and the whole matter therefore weighed heavily as President Monroe worked his way up to that fateful December 2.

This was the first crisis which prompted President Monroe to speak his mind. Concurrently with it, another, far graver situation was developing. Like most of the difficulties which beset America's foreign relations of the times, this one also was part and parcel of the machinations of the "Unholy Alliance."

9

ENGLAND HAD NOT JOINED the Holy Alliance, and as time passed she became increasingly alienated from it for a number of reasons. Slowly and painfully the English people over the centuries were moving in the direction of a democratic form of government. The Magna Carta, a functioning Parliament, constantly diminishing rights of the King, freedom of speech, curbs on absolute authority, guilds, unions—all were indications of increasing liberty. By 1823 the British were very progressive and liberal compared to the peoples of continental Europe.

There were other powerful reasons which made Britain uneasy over the aims of the Holy Alliance—very practical reasons. England favored a balance of power in Europe, with her diplomats eternally playing one side against the other. The Alliance was destroying this balance as its members acted in concert. Power became more and more concentrated instead of diffused. Most of all, England was uneasy about trade and, because of this, was unalterably opposed to any attempt to recapture the lost Spanish colonies, either to be returned to Spain or set up as monarchies under princelings chosen by the Alliance. This system, with its restrictions on free trade, was intolerable to a nation of sailors and merchants, and Britain had no desire to see it imposed once again in the New World. English traders had lost no time in taking full advantage of the new order of freedom in Latin America. By 1823 an extremely prosperous two-way trade had developed, and England had no intentions of abandoning this commerce, which she surely would have had to do if the former colonies were in any way returned to their old status.

The British Foreign Secretary, Lord Castlereagh, who was quite a stuffy monarchist and conservative, died shortly after the Congress of Verona, which the Alliance had called to consider the reconquest of Latin America. A member of Parliament, George Canning, was appointed in his place, and apparently with an eye to the future, he appointed his trusted cousin, Stratford Canning, as British Minister to Washington.

George Canning had no high ideals about the Holy Alliance, or the rights of European royalty in general. He lived and breathed economics. He was from the great port of Liverpool, and there wasn't much he didn't know about British foreign trade. Canning was no particular friend of the United States either. If he had no high ideas about royalty, neither did he have about America. He was an English "gentleman" to the tips of his toes, cold and arrogant in his conviction of British superiority.

But now a thaw appeared. George Canning had something in mind that required America to be softened up. In a letter to the British Minister in Paris, which "somehow" found its way to Washington, Canning mentioned the "late" Spanish colonies and solemnly stated that England had no intention of appropriating the smallest part of them. He added that while the Holy Alliance might make an effort at reconquest, in his opinion such a venture would be a profitless one.

Such an attitude was welcome in America, and Cousin Stratford was happily able to report to London that the British were "almost popular" in America. Even the suspicious John Quincy Adams played along with the diplomatic game and handily lobbed the ball back to Canning in "comparing their ideas and purposes together, with a view to the accommodation of great interests upon which they had hitherto differed."

The next move was up to Canning, and the opportunity was soon presented as a gentle opening gambit by the American Minister to England, George Rush. In a seemingly casual conversation on August 16, 1823, Rush commented favorably on Britain's opposition to the Holy Alliance and to France's invasion of Spain to restore Ferdinand. He added that if the French Armies were successful, at least there was the consolation that "Great Britain would not allow France to go farther and stop the progress of emancipation in the colonies."

Canning and Rush now began a series of very frank and important conferences which were to shape the final form of the Monroe Doctrine as it was proclaimed a few months later. Canning proposed to Rush that England and the United States join forces to block any designs of the Holy Alliance in Latin America. He did not think that the use of force would be necessary, writing that "the knowledge that the United States being opposed, as well as Great Britain, could not fail to have its influence in checking France's steps."

The proposal was flattering and the complexities were enormous. In spite of Canning's efforts to get a definite answer, Rush stalled, reporting to Washington in detail on each conversation. These reports started arriving in America early in October, and by November the issues were clear. An unprecedented peril confronted the leaders of America. There were three separate but closely related problems. Each had to be solved.

The first was that of Russia and her schemes in the Pacific.

The second was that of the Holy Alliance and its schemes in Latin America. In connection with this a decision had to be made on England's offer of cooperation.

And third, there must at long last be a general statement of America's position of isolation incorporated with the answers to the specific problems.

Many of the giants of America's early days were still alive, and James Monroe did not fail to take full advantage of their wisdom. Instinctively he wrote to Thomas Jefferson, unyielding believer in democracy, and to James Madison, the "Father of the Constitution," asking their valued opinions. Both were very elderly and retired, but they took the time to perform one more act on behalf of the country they loved so deeply.

In his covering letter, Monroe outlined briefly the situation, discussing the pros and cons, and concluding with his own opinion, which in view of the final statement of the Doctrine is surprising.

October 17, 1823

" . . . My own impression is that we ought to meet the proposals of the British government, and to make it known that we would view any interference on the part of the European powers, and especially an attack on the colonies by them as an attack on ourselves. . . . I am sensible, however, of the extent and difficulty of the question and shall be happy to have yours and Mr. Madison's opinions on it.

I do not wish to trouble either of you with small objects, but the present one is vital, involving the high interests for which we have so long and so faithfully and harmoniously contended together. Be so kind as to enclose to him the dispatches, with an intimation of the motive."

"With great respect and regard, I am, dear, sir,
Your friend,
James Monroe"

Jefferson lost no time in answering. His letter is dated October 24, 1823.

"Dear Sir:

"The question presented by the letters you have [sent] me is the most momentous which has ever been offered to my contemplation since that of independence which made us a nation . . . .

"While [Europe] is laboring to become the domicile of despotism, our endeavor should surely be to make our hemisphere that of freedom.

"One nation, most of all, could disturb us in this pursuit. . . . Great Britain is the nation which can do us the most harm of anyone . . . on earth; and with her on our side we [need] not fear the whole world. . . . Not that I would purchase even her amity at the price of taking part in her wars. But the war in which the present proposition might engage us, should that be its consequence, is not her war, but ours. . . .

"But I am clearly of Mr. Canning's opinion that it will prevent, instead of provoking war. . . .

"I should think it, therefore, advisable that the Executive should encourage the British government to a continuance of the dispositions expressed in these letters. . . .

"I add the assurance of my constant affectionate friendship and respect.

Thomas Jefferson."

James Madison also lost no time in answering Monroe's appeal for advice. His letter is dated October 30, 1823, and, like Jefferson, he analyzed the situation clearly and without hesitation.

". . . It is particularly fortunate that the policy of Great Britain, although guided by calculations different than ours, has presented a co-operation for an object the same as ours. With that co-operation we have nothing to fear from the rest of Europe; and with it the best reliance on success to our just and laudable views. There ought not be any backwardness therefore, I think, in meeting her the way she has proposed, keeping in view of course, the spirit and forms of the Constitution in every step, if those short of war should be without avail. . . .

"I return the correspondence of Mr. R. and Mr. C. with assurances of the highest respect and sincere regard.

James Madison"

On November 7, 1823, Monroe began a series of meetings with his Cabinet. From the very first, wide differences of opinion were painfully apparent, with Monroe sitting in the middle trying to sift kernels of truth from each. On one side was fiery John C. Calhoun, the Secretary of War and one of the "War Hawks" of 1812. With him was William Wirt, Attorney General, who had first gained national fame for presenting the government's position during the treason trial of Aaron Burr in 1807. They were convinced that there was not a moment to waste; they advocated quick action. Opposing them was John Quincy Adams, Secretary of State and advocate of moderation.

As the meetings progressed, each side became more vehement.

"Mr. President," said John Calhoun, "in my mind there is no doubt that the Holy Alliance plans immediate conquest of the lost Spanish colonies in Latin America."

"And once those colonies are retaken," snapped Wirt, "then the United States is next in line."

Monroe wearily passed his hand over his forehead and looked at his Secretary of State. "And your opinion, Mr. Adams?"

Said Adams, "I no more believe that the Holy Alliance will restore the Spanish dominion upon the American continent than that Chimborazo will sink beneath the waves."

"How can you be so sure?" cried Calhoun.

"The distances are too great. They won't waste blood and treasure in the attempt. If they did, and *if* they succeeded, what then? It is not possible that Britain would acquiesce in any such division of spoils."

Calhoun snorted and looked at Wirt in disgust.

"But the French have just taken Cadiz in Spain," interposed President Monroe, "and it is a natural jumping-off place from which to mount an invasion across the Atlantic."

(Later, Adams was to write in his diary that "President Monroe is alarmed beyond anything I would have conceived possible. And as for Calhoun, he is perfectly moonstruck at the danger.")

And still the talks went on.

"But suppose," said Monroe, "the danger from the Holy Alliance is lesser, or greater, than some of us imagine, would it not at least be prudent to accept the offer of cooperation from England?"

"You are correct, Sir," answered Calhoun. "In any event, come what may, such an alliance will minimize the danger to us."

Monroe looked at Adams and smiled. He knew his Secretary of State well. "And you, Mr. Adams? Do you also take the opposite point of view?"

Adams said, "Indeed I do. I mistrust the English. Their real purpose, as always, is self-interest. They wish to obtain a commitment from us and then do with it as they will. Remember, our cousins act only from motives of trade. Remember this. What possible interest could they have for the restoration of European commercial monopolies in Latin America?"

There was silence for a moment, then Adams banged his fist on the table. "My belief, gentlemen, is that this nation can go its own way and it is high time to say so. This affords a suitable and convenient opportunity to take our stand against the Holy Alliance, and at the same time to decline the overture from Great Britain. It would be more candid as well as more dignified to avow our principles explicitly to Russia and France than to come in as a cockboat in the wake of the British man-of-war."

Monroe gazed quietly at Adams. "Yes," he half mused, "but that is only an opinion, Mr. Adams. *I* must do what is necessary, and I cannot tamper with the security of the United States on the basis of an *opinion.*"

Adams looked down at the table a moment, then back up at his chief. "No, you cannot, Sir," was all he said.

Slowly President Monroe made up his mind. He came to accept Adams' point of view but stuck to his own guns, judging the risk too great to do otherwise, since it *was possible* that the Holy Alliance would attack Latin America and hence needed to be warned. He drafted a first message, and it contained the heart of what the Monroe Doctrine was to be.

"I believe, Mr. President," said Adams, "it is too strong."

For once Adams and Wirt were in agreement.

"We cannot defy all of Europe in language that is practically a summons to arms," said Wirt.

"Correct," said Adams.

"Nor can we assume an attitude of menace without meaning to strike," continued Wirt.

Adams nodded in agreement, then addressed President Monroe forcefully. "I still do not think the danger of an invasion of Latin America by the Holy Alliance is great. But if you do, Sir, let us not throw it menacingly in anyone's face. A stand, yes. Say what you mean. Let the record be straight. If war *should* come, we'll not too soon take our stand to repel it."

As Monroe pondered, wrestling with the agony of making the decision, no doubt he must have considered the words of a friend long dead—George Washington. Washington was fondly remembered by Monroe not just as a close personal acquaintance, but as a great patriot, clear-thinking and utterly reliable. It surely must have been natural for him to recall the words of the first President's Farewell Address: "If we remain one people under an efficient government, the period is not far off when we can defy material injury from external annoyance; when we may take such an attitude as will cause the neutrality which we may at times resolve upon to be scrupulously respected; when belligerent nations, under the impossibility of making acquisitions upon us, choose peace, or war, as our interests, guided by justice, may counsel."

In the early days of American independence, the issues had seemed very clear: freedom, the rights of man. Americans had not hesitated then, though the odds were strong against them. Now, in 1823, Monroe must have felt that he could do no less than follow the same path. He made up his mind, no longer hesitating. The gauntlet must be thrown down to those who would attack liberty. America must stand on her own two feet as champion of freedom.

By November 26, 1823, the final draft of the message was written. Before Congress and the whole world the words of James Monroe were to ring clearly. The Tsar could go to the devil, along with the Holy Alliance. The country had no need of any pact with Great Britain, nor were the phrases minced regarding how America felt about other people meddling in its business or the business of the New World.

Considering the background and all the fuss, the reaction was not extreme or warlike. It was, in fact, something of a deflation.

Chateaubriand, the French Foreign Secretary, said, "It ought to be resisted by all the powers possessing either territorial or commercial interests in that hemisphere." *L'Etoile*, the great French newspaper, commented caustically that it was "ridiculous that a republic only forty years old . . . should take all of the Americas under her control."

Holy Alliance high priest Metternich delivered the opinion that the message was about what could be expected from nations adhering to republican principles. He sourly enlarged upon "the calamities that would be brought to Europe by the establishment of these vast republics in the New World."

Tsar Alexander was a bit more upset. He mumbled and sulked angrily and tried his futile best to convince the Holy

Alliance that something should be done. He finally settled his own problems by diplomacy, drawing back to the already established Russian colonies in Alaska and concluding a treaty with Great Britain which set the boundary between Canada and Alaska about where it is now.

Down in California, Fort Ross slid into twilight. It had been a pretty little place with orchards, gardens and lush fields—a charming oasis of aristocratic culture with elegant officers, a lovely blond princess, a piano, French wines and a conservatory for flowers. The sea otters had almost been exterminated, and there was no longer any reason for its existence. Americans were beginning to move into Alta California, and the Russians were no match for these aggressive and hungry land-seekers. The Russian-American Trading Company gave up the ghost and sold out lock, stock and barrel to John Sutter in 1842. This same John Sutter later discovered gold in California and set off an entirely new chapter in the history of the West.

England's reaction to the message was more complicated. At first Canning was jubilant. He wrote to the British Minister in Spain that the "Congress of Verona was broken in all its limbs before, but the President's speech gives it the *coup de grace*."

Canning's pleasure turned to chagrin, however, as the matter developed. He had been outmaneuvered diplomatically. The United States already recognized the independence of the new Latin-American nations. Britain had not yet done so and the speech in a way spiked England's guns, setting the United States up as the protector of freedom in the New World, a position that Canning had very much wanted to develop for England. Monroe's message twanged British nerves painfully.

Actually Canning needn't have worried much about Britain's stance in Latin America. Monroe's principles were well received there, as was the promptness with which the United States had acknowledged the independence of the new states. However, America's neighbors were highly practical. They had no illusions about where real world power lay in those years. It was in England and not in the United States. If the time came when a protector was needed, Great Britain would be a far more effective one.

About the only truly enthusiastic comment on Monroe's message was that of the venerable Marquis de Lafayette. Lafayette was an honorary American citizen and a sturdy believer in democracy. In the face of general European apathy to the speech, Lafayette exulted and was moved to write that it was "the best little bit of paper that God has ever permitted any man to give to the world."

If the general reaction abroad ranged from tepid acclaim to irritation or contempt, the opposite was true in the United States. Forcefully and publicly, the American President had echoed the sentiments of his countrymen. He had expressed a doctrine in which the people believed—the doctrine of freedom. Americans were deeply stirred. They were proud of their President, of themselves, of their country.

The British Minister in Washington gauged American reaction precisely. In a dispatch home he reported that "The message seems to have been received with acclamation throughout the United States. . . . The explicit and manly tone . . . has evidently found in every bosom a chord which vibrates in strict unison with the sentiments so conveyed. It would indeed be difficult in a country composed of elements so various, and liable on all subjects to opinions so conflicting, to find more perfect unanimity than has been displayed on every side on this particular point."

In December of 1823, there was no doubt as to how Americans felt about freedom and about their country. The times were perilous, the dangers enormous, but the people were united in love for the United States of America and in their willingness to stand behind it in the cause of freedom and justice.

10

THE PUBLIC STATEMENT of the principles expressed in James Monroe's message to Congress was an important step forward in the development of the United States of America. The declaration before the whole world of America's dedication to freedom, backed up by action if necessary, was a gratifying sign of manhood.

What developed, however, was more like wavering adolescence. Europe still was not done with the New World, and in spite of its brave and stirring words, the United States apparently was not interested.

On at least four occasions between 1823 and 1826, various Latin-American governments sent diplomatic envoys scurrying to Washington in the hope that the noble phrases of Monroe's could be used effectively to protect them from continual European threats and harassment.

One of these cases even involved a powerful French invasion force cruising off the coast of Haiti. In masterful examples of diplomatic doubletalk the United States made the point to its frantic Latin-American neighbors that it didn't want to be bothered. The French sailed back home again for reasons of their own, not because of anything America did or said.

Lack of American cooperation or interest was evident in other fields, too. For example, one of the great dreams of Simón Bolívar had been that of establishing some sort of a union of the free nations of the Western Hemisphere. This union was not to have been political or military, but more of a mutual assistance agreement to promote advancement in the fields of peace—medicine, education, art, commerce. Thus, more than 125 years ahead of his time, Bolívar, the "impractical dreamer," foresaw the day when such a union would be established with the United States a willing partner. But in 1826 the U.S. Government wouldn't even discuss the matter and went so far as to refuse to send delegates as observers to the Congress which Bolívar called in Panama.

Throughout the 1830s also there were a large number of "violations" of Monroe's message. England, particularly, did just about as she pleased in the Western Hemisphere. She established small colonies and trading outposts and in general promoted her own interests in any way that seemed convenient. She meddled openly in Argentina. She seized the Falkland Islands. Crown colonies were set up in Central America, and considerable portions of what are now Honduras and Nicaragua were smoothly annexed.

In those days Central America was still one nation. The territory had not yet split up, and so once more in desperation a Central American diplomat made a hasty trip to Washington to ask for help in combating the British land grabs. The trip was fruitless.

In closing conversations with Andrew Jackson's Secretary of State, the envoy rather plaintively said, "Suffer me to remind you that it has always been the policy of the United

States that there should be no European settlements on the American continent."

The Secretary of State seemed a bit bored with the whole business. He thought for a moment and then replied, "It is not deemed expedient to interfere in the matter."

Discussions and debates in the government and by people in the street seemed to serve only one purpose—they kept alive the memory of Monroe's words, and this was all. The import of the message was forgotten—dead. Nevertheless, the hopes and dreams of the American people, which had been so resoundingly expressed, were *not* dead. By the 1840s they began to show signs of revival and to be quoted as though there were still something in them which people believed.

When 180 Texas volunteers under the command of Cols. James Bowie and William B. Travis made their heroic but futile defense of the Alamo against 4,000 soldiers commanded by the Mexican General Antonio Santa Anna, a struggle was set off which ended in the revival of the message of Monroe! The Alamo fell in 1836 after twelve desperate days of fighting. These twelve days were enough for Col. Sam Houston to perfect plans for the defense of Texas. When freedom for the huge territory was finally won, Texas immediately applied for admission to the United States.

The question was far from a simple one, as Texas was a slaveholding territory; already the nation was taking the entire matter of slavery very seriously. The Senate debated the matter for eight long years, and during this time both France and England made very determined efforts to keep Texas out of the Union. In so doing they hoped to "divide" the continent of North America and achieve the start of a balance of power situation. While the problem was heatedly argued pro and con, a rather surprising thing took place. Monroe's message came to life! It was widely quoted and recalled as the people of the entire nation looked for a principle upon which they could hang their objection to European meddling in the affairs of the continent.

During this period also, the questions of the Oregon Territory and of California provided further opportunities for the principles expressed by Monroe to be revived and be used to the hilt in backing a stand by the Government. President James Polk minced no words. In an interpretation of the message that left no doubt in anybody's mind about how Americans felt, he warned foreign nations, particularly Great Britain, to stay out of the Pacific Northwest.

Polk's use of Monroe's message also made clear one other very important point—a point that in later years was to come in for much bitter criticism. The principles expressed by Monroe were *unilateral.* Their interpretation and application were up to the United States *alone.* They would be applied only where and how America wished. If the government decided to ignore "violations" in one place, at one time, this by no means meant that it would ignore them elsewhere, at another time.

This policy of unilateral interpretation permitted the nation to overlook many infringements in Latin America during the period from the end of President Polk's term of office to about the time of the Civil War. One of these infringements even involved a British punitive fleet sailing right up the River Plate in Argentina. The United States chose to look the other way. The idea of isolation on America's own terms was becoming more and more rooted in American life and government. There were two exceptions to this policy during these years.

Although the time was far distant when the Panama Canal would be built, already people were thinking about it. Vaguely they felt that when the time came for its construction, it must be an "American" canal. The two exceptions to the isolationist feeling had to do with the initial skirmishing over the future waterway.

At this time the Isthmus of Panama was a province of the Republic of Colombia, and the first exception was a treaty that America signed with that nation, which aimed gingerly at some vague point in the distant future when a canal might be built. America granted Colombia many concessions, including those accorded a "favored nation."

The other exception was with Great Britain, also skirting around the edges of the subject of a future canal. The confusion and the argument which surrounded this treaty were typical of the uncertainty which still existed when it came to the application of Monroe's message.

England had begun to be overly ambitious in acquiring bases which easily could in the future serve as terminals for a canal in Nicaragua to connect the Atlantic and Pacific. People in America cried out that our interests were at stake in permitting England to go ahead with her plans and that the whole thing was a danger to American isolation as well as a violation of the principles expressed by Monroe.

Accordingly, the Government negotiated a treaty with Great Britain—the famous Clayton-Bulwer Treaty. Now, *others* insisted that *this* treaty was a violation of the precious principles of Monroe! Actually, the whole matter was a tempest in a teapot.

America did not invoke Monroe's message, or insist that England get out, or any other such thing. There was no need to. The treaty was neither a military nor a political alliance. America had merely joined with the English in promising not to occupy, fortify or colonize the territories in question. And, since the Panama Canal was finally built on territory which had been a part of Colombia, the problems as they arose were with that nation and the newly independent Republic of Panama, not with England or Nicaragua.

So it was that in spite of a long slumber, in various ways the principles in Monroe's message came to life. They did so frequently enough, and with sufficient force, that they were not completely forgotten. Also, for the first time during these years, the term "doctrine" began to be used instead of simpler and vaguer words, such as "speech," or "principle," or "message."

The use of the word "doctrine" was a good indication of the direction that the growth of Monroe's speech was taking. Anything which is a doctrine conveys a religious feeling, a feeling of something which is deep and ingrained. And as this began to happen, in people's minds the Monroe Doctrine started to be cloaked with a powerful, almost mystical aura. Right or wrong, good or bad, just or unjust, the application of the Doctrine or anything to do with it became dogma, became a matter for heated, violent discussion.

As a doctrine, the principles of Monroe became a basic tenet of America's foreign policy, officially and in the minds of ordinary citizens. Though the Doctrine might be derided in Europe, only weakly mentioned in official dispatches and never as yet used as a strong, threatening stick, it was nevertheless becoming more and more important to America. As the nation was growing, so was the Monroe Doctrine awakening and beginning to flex its muscles. The United States of America and the Monroe Doctrine had both developed to where they could face up to a real challenge. It was not long in coming.

The Civil War was a mortal threat to the survival of the nation. During the years of the War, and after its conclusion, came the first big test of the principles of the Monroe Doctrine.

Since the time of Metternich and the machinations of the Holy Alliance, the governments of the Old World had steadily become more antidemocratic and absolute. The seeds of despotic power which had sprouted so vigorously continued to flourish. Hatred of democratic institutions in Europe grew by leaps and bounds. Revolt after revolt in suffering and oppressed Old World kingdoms was crushed with ever-increasing ferocity. It was as though the entire aristocratic system knew it was fighting for its life and was determined to survive. With this, Europe's kings never ceased to dream of re-establishing power in Latin America.

All too often their meddling found fertile ground because, in general, the young republics of Latin America were having a very difficult time. The sad, prophetic words of the dying Bolívar that "those who had served the revolution had ploughed the sea" were often true. In too many countries freedom was a meaningless word leading to chaos, granting permission to repress helpless minorities or to confer favor and privileges upon the rich and strong. America's neighbors to the south were having a hard time learning to govern themselves.

The most stable, efficient and decent government in South America was that of Brazil—still governed by a royalty which was an offshoot of the Portuguese monarchy. Little wonder that there were many honest and sincere men in Latin America who believed that the masses of people were not capable of governing themselves. They were certain that the best governments were those headed by responsible ruling families. Even though such systems were sure to bring evils, anything was better than the confusion which existed in many Latin-American states. Such sentiments naturally found sympathetic audiences in the courts of Europe.

One more powerful fact stimulated these royal European schemers and opportunists who so hungrily eyed Latin America. This fact was the undeniably spectacular growth of the United States. America was proving that democracy could work. Daily its power increased. Daily its influence, whether anybody liked it or not, was growing in Latin America. This political and commercial stability and growing influence gave strong comfort to those who believed in democracy and likewise frightened those who believed only in kings and despotism. The latter realized full well that if empires were ever again to be established in Latin America, royalty would have to move quickly.

Accordingly, England, Spain and France decided upon a plan to place a monarch on a throne in Mexico. Mexico was logical because it was the country closest to the United States and therefore the most likely to be infected with the "sickness" of democracy from north of its border. It was the most logical place for the United States to expand, hence in the greatest "danger" if, as according to many in Europe, America had plans for the establishment of a vast economic and political "kingdom" of its own in the Western Hemisphere. On top of all this, Mexico had been currently going through such an agony of revolution and disorder that its people quite reasonably might welcome a little stability in government for a change.

This "invasion" of the New World was confusing. The original partners were Spain, France and England. As it worked out, Spain invaded Santo Domingo, France invaded Mexico and England pulled out of the whole venture.

The time was well chosen for the invaders. Even with foreign troops swarming into the Caribbean and Mexico, there was little the United States could do at the moment.

The country was engaged in a bitter Civil War. Its life hung in the balance. The commitment was so desperate that the Government and the people had no time or thought for anything else—Spain, England, France or the Monroe Doctrine.

The Mexican people astonished the French by demonstrating that they knew how to fight, and die if necessary, in defense of their homeland. They didn't value aristocratic order and stability as highly as had been hoped. Nevertheless, in spite of fierce opposition, French troops were in Mexico City by 1863. The "throne" of Mexico was offered by France to the Austrian Archduke, Maximilian. He accepted, was installed with great pomp as Emperor and, with his wife Carlotta as Queen, set up business south of America's border. The Government of the United States was busy with Vicksburg, and many other Civil War battlefields. It could do little more than protest the establishment of this Latin-American kingdom, and feebly at that.

Nobody was fooling anybody, however. The European princes and kings and chancellors were realists if nothing else. Maximilian was nervous on his throne. The Government of France, which supported him, was nervous. Nobody in his right mind doubted that eventually order would be restored within the borders of the United States. And then the big question—what would America do about this monarchy in Mexico, which was supported only by French muskets and bayonets?

When the Civil War was finally ended, no one was left in doubt. There was a dogma in the United States, and it was called the "Monroe Doctrine." It was proclaimed immediately and forcefully. After all the years since its proclamation, suddenly America's precious Doctrine revealed that it had real meaning. It was the perfect peg on which to hang objections to Maximilian.

The pressure which the American State Department brought was all against France, not against Mexico or the by now very shaky monarchy of the hapless Austrian Archduke. The pressure was strong but very simple and direct. The language of diplomacy was elegant and polite, but the message was clear: "France, get out of Mexico. Go home." Nobody had any illusions about what would happen in Mexico once the French troops were removed.

French officials took a quick look at the United States. They saw a nation ablaze with pride and martial spirit at the conclusion of the Civil War. They saw a nation which for the first time in its history was fully aware of the steel and cannon and men it could muster if the need arose. France wanted no part of an engagement with such an adversary. By January of 1866, the matter was settled. France withdrew her troops.

In Mexico, however, matters were not so simple. Maximilian was abandoned to the tender mercies of his Mexican subjects. During his reign he had been dissolute, corrupt, arrogant—a foolish, imperial dreamer. The only thing he managed to do with dignity during his entire unhappy time in Mexico was to die with courage before the guns of a Mexican firing squad.

Maximilian's royal consort, Carlotta, was the daughter of a Belgian king and a French princess. She was a storybook queen—beautiful, regal, loyal. In another era she might have lived a useful and happy life, but in Mexico she was in the wrong place at the wrong time. When things began going badly for Maximilian, she returned to Europe and put up a gallant fight for help and for justice as she saw it. She traveled from one court to another, battling stubbornly and fiercely for aid to her forlorn monarch-husband in far-off Mexico. But none of the kings of the Old World wanted anything to do with this rattlesnake's nest in the

Western Hemisphere. The cause of monarchy was lost. Carlotta's efforts were useless. When Maximilian was executed in 1867, her reason failed. She was cared for in a religious institution until she died in 1927.

Without firm American diplomatic action, Maximilian and his ill-starred kingdom might have been doomed in any event. Even its backers in Europe had been from the very start uncertain about the venture. There is no doubt, however, that the pressure from the United States, inspired by the principles of the Monroe Doctrine, was an important factor in its downfall.

Just as important, but less dramatic, was the Spanish invasion of Santo Domingo.

After Santo Domingo's independence from Spain was proclaimed, the so-called leaders of the republic found it increasingly difficult to control the seething island. Each of many different factions fought bitterly with the others in efforts to dominate and exploit the recently liberated people. Utter chaos was the result. Finally, those people who were still loyal to Spain took advantage of the confusion and appealed to nearby Cuba for aid. Cuba was still a Spanish colony, and the governor was happy to oblige. With the United States desperately involved in the Civil War, he felt no fear when he dispatched Spanish troops to Santo Domingo. The invasion was easy and completely successful, and very shortly peace of the monarchical order reigned once more. The island fell back in the fold as a royal colony of the empire of Spain.

William H. Seward, the American Secretary of State, was far too busy to do much more than protest mildly at the French invasion of Mexico, but for some reason this was not the case with that of the Spanish in Santo Domingo. A series of extremely sharp notes and threats was exchanged between Washington and Madrid. Seward made certain, in very strong language, that the Spanish Government knew without any doubt how the United States felt about Santo Domingo and its forced return to the status of a Spanish colony. Furthermore, he did this under the waving banner of the Monroe Doctrine. This was the first time that the Doctrine as such had ever been invoked as an instrument of American foreign policy. During all the note-exchanging with France over Maximilian in Mexico, the Monroe Doctrine had not been mentioned by name. Its principles had been invoked but the term itself was not used. Not so in Santo Domingo! The Spanish occupation was called an outright violation of America's Monroe Doctrine.

The results were not impressive. The Spanish Government angrily inquired as to just what was this Monroe Doctrine! Spanish diplomats had never heard of it, so they said. In any event, they couldn't have cared less. Spanish troops had been sent to Santo Domingo at the express invitation of the people of that island. They had every intention of staying. In very blunt language, Madrid asked what the United States of America intended doing.

The United States intended to do nothing! It was too busy with a devastating war at home. Out of the exchange of notes a great lesson was learned by the American Government. Nobody would pay any attention to the Monroe Doctrine or to any other noble and resounding statement of rights and policies unless force was available to back it up with action if need be. In this case, no force was available. America backed water and got on with its problems at home.

Other events settled the matter. By 1865 there were some 25,000 Spanish troops in Santo Domingo energetically doing their best to persuade the people that the royal monarchy of Spain was the best of all possible governments. They didn't have much luck. Guerrilla warfare, hatred of the people in general and yellow fever dogged them from the start. At the end of the Civil War the American Government would have been able to take up the problem in earnest, with plenty of power to back up its position. Spain came to the conclusion that it wanted no part of such a struggle. In the same year that soldiers were being mustered out of the Union Army, Spanish troops were being evacuated from Santo Domingo.

These two episodes—that of the French under Louis Napoleon, with its sponsorship of the ill-fated Maximilian in Mexico, and the return of Spain to Santo Domingo—were immensely important in the development of the Monroe Doctrine.

Whether it had been decisive in forcing the French from Mexico or the Spanish from Santo Domingo will never be known for sure. One thing, however, was known. From this point onward, the Doctrine was recognized throughout all the courts of Europe as a definite statement of policy of the United States of America. As such, in the future it was to be heavily weighed and considered in the chancelleries of the world when problems arose concerning the Western Hemisphere.

11

ONE OF GERMANY'S MOST FAMOUS MEN of the past was Otto von Bismarck, the great "iron chancellor." He was the chief architect and planner of his country's rise to world power near the end of the 1890s. This stern Prussian militarist was tolerant of no interference when it came to anybody or anything standing in the way of German might and expansion.

Bismarck took one look at the words of a speech that had been given in America in 1823 and snarled, ". . . the Monroe Doctrine is a species of arrogance peculiarly American and inexcusable. It is a specter that would vanish in plain daylight."

He could not have been more wrong.

One of the main points in Monroe's statement was, of course, that the United States would not permit any foreign nation to establish new colonies in the Western Hemisphere. During the period from the end of the Civil War to about the turn of the century, there were no problems of this sort. No European government made any attempt to gain new footholds in the New World.

This perhaps wasn't because of any lack of basic desire to do so, or even possibly because of any real fear of the United States, if the matter had ever come to a showdown. There was another, completely different reason. France, England, Holland, Belgium and a unified, swiftly arming Germany were too busy in other parts of the globe.

These were the years of the great European colonial expansions. Vast and incredibly rich overseas empires were being forged. Africa, the whole enormous Near East and the Orient were falling like ripe plums to the greedy businessmen, the rabid nationalists and the powerful armies and navies of Europe. Few countries had the inclination, the time or the resources to bother with some fever-ridden, poverty-stricken little out-at-the-elbows former Spanish colony in Central or South America. Unbelievable fortunes and lands and glory were waiting for the easy grabbing elsewhere.

So America over these years had no troubles with foreign troops conquest-bound in the New World. There were occasional incidents, of course, but they were of no great importance in themselves. They served mainly to keep the Doctrine alive, and to permit it to be more and more liberally interpreted to cover a widening array of situations. There was nothing wrong with this; it was a simple matter of growth and development of the Doctrine.

By the end of the century, however, the great world empires had been pretty well established. There was little left to grab. Once again Europe began to pay more attention to the political, commercial and territorial empty spaces in Latin America. By now, the United States and its Monroe Doctrine were ready for them!

In 1895 Great Britain became embroiled in a violent dispute with Venezuela over the boundary line between that free nation and the neighboring British colony of Guiana. Britain threatened military action if she did not get her way.

President Grover Cleveland took a very firm stand. In a most positive and uncompromising challenge to England he stated that the United States would resist by every means in its power ". . . appropriation by Great Britain of any lands or the exercise of governmental jurisdiction over any territory which after investigation we had determined of right belongs to Venezuela."

England took a careful look at the New World and the United States of America and decided it didn't want any part of such an argument over a steaming jungle boundary line. The matter was submitted to arbitration.

And so it was that the implications in the Monroe Doctrine were extended. America would not only object to the acquisition of new European colonies in the Western Hemisphere but would also protest vigorously any juggling of ownership or boundaries. This stand would be backed up by arms if necessary. Thus the foundation for a whole new concept of the broader meaning of isolationism was established.

In 1902 another event took place, and out of it still another interpretation of the Monroe Doctrine evolved. The interpretation was novel but nevertheless completely logical and inevitable. Although no one was aware of it at the time, this extension of the Doctrine was in an ominous direction. Ultimately it brought down on America's head more ill feeling and criticism than any other act in the country's history.

The event in itself was simple enough.

An exceptionally obnoxious dictator in Venezuela named Cipriano Castro was in deep financial trouble. He was seven years behind on the interest on money which had been lent to him by German bankers. He had never paid any dividends on a flourishing railroad which Germans had financed in his country. He had made no effort to compensate German citizens living in Venezuela for their property, which had been destroyed or grabbed outright in the revolution which brought him to power.

All in all, Castro was in real difficulties with his finances. England, Italy, some other European nations and the United States as well were lined up along with the principal creditor, Germany, for the collection of money due. Germany was the first nation to announce intentions of doing something about the situation. She sent a note to the American Government and outlined the plan which she intended to follow.

This plan involved a blockade of Venezuelan ports and the seizure of Venezuelan gunboats. If this did not work, then Germany would "consider the occupation of Venezuelan harbors and the levying of duties in those places." Germany was quite obviously out to collect the money, and the most effective way to do it was by collecting duties on imports and exports.

The American Government reacted quite calmly to the note. Secretary of State John Hay replied that "The Monroe Doctrine is a declaration that there must be no territorial aggrandizement by any non-American power at the expense of any American power on American soil. The Doctrine had nothing to do with commercial relations of any American power. We do not guarantee any state against punishment if it misconducts itself. . . ." There was a good deal more to Secretary Hay's reply to Germany, but it was all to the effect that the Monroe Doctrine was concerned only with the acquisition of territory by a foreign power.

Hay had not reckoned with the temper and mood of his

countrymen. A storm broke in America. The American people made their voices heard, and they spoke different words from those used by the Department of State! If the United States Government was willing to allow foreign warships and troops in Venezuela, this by no means meant that the American people were happy about it. No matter what the reason for the presence of those ships and troops, Americans didn't like it. There was the Monroe Doctrine to be considered as far as they were concerned.

All in all, there was perhaps good reason for suspicion in America. Over the previous five years Germany had been building a large and modern navy. She needed bases and coaling stations in the Western Hemisphere. Admiral Von Tirpitz openly advocated that Germany secure by any means necessary such bases in the Danish West Indies, in Curaçao, in Brazil, in the Galapagos or even in Dutch Guiana. The German Kaiser himself had said that what was best for the Imperial Navy must be done, "even if it displeases the Yankees."

Pressure from the American people forced the State Department to query Germany more closely about this venture in Venezuela. The German Foreign Office replied that the intentions were pure. All Germany wanted was to collect the money due. "The reports that are circulated concerning German plans for conquest in South and Central America are lies and slanders of our enemies."

Americans didn't believe such pious statements. Germany was hungry for overseas possessions and colonies. She had been tardy arriving at the international colonial banquet. Unification of many small, quarreling states into one powerful modern nation had come later in Germany than in other European countries. While the colonial grabbing had been really good, Germany had been unable to do much about it. When she was ready, the choicest cuts at the table already were gobbled up.

What was more natural, most Americans argued, than for Germany to use this Venezuelan money business to gain a permanent foothold in Spanish America? The strong principle upon which Americans based their determination to stop such a thing was the Monroe Doctrine. Furthermore, they knew that the German Government had little or no respect for it. Little wonder that Americans were suspicious past the point of being calm about the whole matter when a powerful fleet of German, Italian and British ships steamed into position off the coast of Venezuela on December 9, 1902. And, to cap it all and to add vastly to the confusion, Venezuela herself now appealed to the United States for help in the sacred name of the Monroe Doctrine!

The feelings of the American people, reflected in the press and in speeches in Congress, were intense. They were not soothed, either, by the continual virulence of the attacks in the German press! Regardless of its original lack of concern, the Government of the United States had to recognize the public temper and take a more serious view of the entire affair.

Theodore Roosevelt was President at the time. In 1916, in letters which he wrote, and again in 1917, in speeches he made, he stated that he had very emphatically called the attention of the German Government to this violation of the Monroe Doctrine. He commented that in a conversation with the German Ambassador in Washington he had said that "if no notification of submission to arbitration came within a certain number of days, I should be obliged to order Dewey to take his fleet to the Venezuelan coast and see that the German forces did not take possession of any territory."

There is no record of any such statement in the diplomatic correspondence of the times. However, in private letters and in private conversations with reliable people, the record is that President Roosevelt did take this forthright stand and did make the statements to Germany which he later recalled. His position on the matter is perfectly clear, and it had results. After Venezuela's appeal for help in the name of the Monroe Doctrine, along with her request that the matter be submitted for arbitration, Germany and the other nations involved immediately backed down. The fleets were withdrawn in 1903, and the entire matter was finally turned over to the Hague in 1904.

The American people and their Monroe Doctrine had triumphed. Notes sent back to the United States from the Foreign Offices of the European nations involved stated over and over again that there had been no intention of interfering with America's interpretation of the Monroe Doctrine. Nothing had been intended by anyone to give offense to the feelings of the United States or its people or to downgrade the Doctrine in any way.

This had been a very clear-cut situation, and there was no confusion regarding the part which the Monroe Doctrine played in it. Other events of the same period, however, did not provoke such definite feelings in the minds of Americans or of foreign nations. In these cases nobody could quite figure out just how much the principles of the Doctrine were or were not involved.

One set of circumstances arose out of the Spanish-American War, which was concluded in 1901. Should America annex or not annex Cuba? The issue was extremely complicated. Some people said yes, and others no. Would it have been a "violation" of the Doctrine for the United States to do what it prohibited others from doing? Cuba, of course, was not annexed. The case of Puerto Rico, which had little or no organized government, was a still different matter. This island did become a territory of the United States, as did the Philippine Islands.

The case of Hawaii, which had taken place a few years previously, in 1898, also was different. The topic provoked a storm in America; the Monroe Doctrine was quoted both for and against annexation. In any event, the islands peacefully became a territory of the United States at the express invitation of the people living there.

In these situations there were no clean lines drawn. Expansionists at home were all for territorial grabs. Anti-expansionists were against them. Each side talked loudly and long and twisted the Monroe Doctrine this way and that to back up its claims. Foreign governments as well screamed to high heaven as *they* interpreted the Doctrine to fit their own feelings about these really quite modest "territorial expansions" of the United States. Each situation, however, was finally resolved on its own merits; basically the Monroe Doctrine was not involved.

Most importantly, though, each of these cases had very little to do with the growth and development of the Doctrine, or with the establishment of any expression of it which was to be applied in the future. The money woes of Cipriano Castro in Venezuela did bear heavily on the Doctrine, however, and the American public knew it. Somehow the people understood that in this situation the heart of the Doctrine was expressed and that in the solution and application of the principles a path was to be outlined for their use in years to come.

For this reason the people of America made the stand they did. As the German press said during the height of the furor, "The attitude of the American public was a truly hysterical demonstration." Hysterical or not, Americans knew how they felt, and they knew where the kernel of their Monroe Doctrine lay. Events were to prove them right, for out of the Venezuelan affair arose circumstances which were to concern America and her neighbors for many, many years.

The application of the Doctrine in these circumstances was to become known as the famous "Roosevelt Corollary" to the Monroe Doctrine. A corollary is something which is a natural consequence, or result. The Roosevelt Corollary was the natural consequence of what the American people had insisted upon during the crisis in Venezuela. It was based upon the completely logical and sound idea that if a person, or a state, has a "right," then also with this right it has a responsibility. In this case it meant that if Venezuela had the right to borrow huge sums of money, then it had the responsibility to make repayment. And for the United States, there was no escaping the fact that if this country had the "right" to keep other countries out of Venezuela when they sought to collect their just debts, then America had the responsibility to see that justice was done.

The position of everybody involved was expressed most clearly in an editorial in the London *Times* in 1903. The editorial no doubt was inspired by America's actions over Venezuela. The *Times* said that "the power which holds the shield over weaker states is under an obligation to compel them to observe their duties to others." These words reflected in no uncertain terms European reaction to America's interpretation of the Monroe Doctrine. What they meant in plain language was that if America would not permit other people to stand up for their rights when weak, small American states misbehaved, then it became America's duty to set matters right. This was not unreasonable.

American reaction to this and, once again, the logical extensions to this reaction were to cause the United States much trouble and bring down on it a great deal of hatred and angry criticism.

The *immediate* cause of all these problems was the action

taken by American citizens and their government in the name of the Monroe Doctrine. But nothing is that simple. Behind this action, and just as much to blame, lay the political and economic systems and the temperaments of many Latin-American states. And even further back, behind this, was the fact that these systems were a direct holdover from the brutal colonialism inflicted on these lands for so many centuries by Spain.

Since the liberation of the Spanish colonies there had been little stability in most of the Latin-American nations. Governments rose and fell, often within days or weeks after coming to power. Each was likely to be more corrupt than that which had preceded it. The common practice was for each aspiring "President" or dictator to finance his regime through large loans in foreign countries. These loans were secured by pledging portions of the customs duties—both on imports and exports. The money borrowed in this way was used to develop mines and to finance railroads, harbor and port facilities, dams, power plants, roads and the like. A considerable part of it also went for arms used to perpetuate the group in control, or directly into the pockets of those in power.

All this was certainly nobody's business except that of the countries involved. The money collected at the custom houses was generally more than ample to finance the loans. The whole system, while corrupt and utterly selfish, worked well enough except for one sad fact of life: the lack of responsibility of the leaders of many of these nations. Too many of them were basically uninterested in making democracy work and unwilling to understand the obligations which inevitably go hand in hand with freedom. There was little in their tradition to prepare them to assume such burdens.

Incoming governments came to control by fraudulent

election or by revolution—the same kind of bloody revolt which had brought their predecessors to power. The new administrations too often had no intentions of honoring the obligations taken on by the government ahead of them, especially since large amounts of the money had been wasted or used to feather private nests. The foreign financiers—banks, individuals, commercial enterprises of one sort or another—quite logically turned to their own governments for help. The request was always the same: take over the collection of customs duties so we can get our money back. This, of course, meant occupation of the big ports by troops or ships.

These lenders might have been unwise. Anyone foolish enough to advance money to such unstable governments, or even invest it in business projects in such mercurial nations, perhaps deserved to lose it. The stakes were enormous, though, and wobbly Latin-American governments had no trouble getting money. The lenders also might have been unrealistic to expect soldiers and warships to be made available to bail them out of the consequences of their greedy lending sprees. All this, however, has little to do with the fact that people who borrow money are expected to repay it, or at least make an effort to do so, and if they don't, to be prepared for trouble in one way or another.

As far as the United States of America was concerned, in such situations there was a terrible trap. Shortsighted though they may have been in making such loans, the creditor nations felt that if they were not allowed to do what was necessary to get their money back because of American adherence to a Doctrine which said that foreign troops were not to be permitted on New World soil, then it had to be up to America to see that justice was done.

There was no escaping the meaning of this. It meant that

America had to supervise the collection of customs duties in the delinquent nations. This is what happened, and it turned the United States, in the name of the Monroe Doctrine—a statement of a principle which was a defense of freedom—into a hated collection agency and armed meddler in other people's affairs.

There was nothing new in the idea as it developed in the early 1900s as the Roosevelt Corollary. Actually, it had been proposed to the United States many times before, notably in 1869 and again in 1881 in connection with that perennial delinquent, Venezuela. Neither Congress nor the American people had been able to stomach any part of it. It meant intervention in the affairs of other free countries and was recognized as containing the seeds of many problems, including even that of the establishment of protectorates.

Now, however, the whole picture was changed. By a series of logical, easy, harmless-appearing steps, this intervention had somehow become part and parcel of something very precious to the American people—the Monroe Doctrine! Strangely enough, *now* armed intervention to collect other people's debts and to establish financial order was not only palatable but proper—even desirable.

This was the Roosevelt Corollary of the Monroe Doctrine. This was the interpretation of the Doctrine which caused the United States so much trouble and which even today causes many nations in Latin America to look northward with hostility and suspicion. They still wonder if "speak softly and carry a big stick" is not really the basis of American foreign policy. They still question "Yankee Imperialism" and "dollar diplomacy."

Whatever the outcome, a course had been set for America. What was to come was logical and inevitable in the light of this new interpretation of the words of James Monroe. And it was to come very swiftly.

Very soon after the United States had made its voice heard regarding the money problems of Venezuela in 1902, and its objection to their solution by Germany, England and Italy, the consequences were upon the country.

12

UNITED STATES MARINES have a reputation for being tough fighting men. They also have a reputation for being outspoken, frequently in language which is as unprintable as it is honest.

Such a Marine was Colonel Smeley Butler. Butler led a good many of the expeditions when Marines were sent into various Latin-American countries to uphold this new interpretation of the Monroe Doctrine. Years later, when he was Commanding General of the Marine Corps, he had this to say about them: "I know that many of these expeditions were nothing but collection trips for the bad debts contracted by Wall Street bankers."

This was the opinion of a very patriotic and honest American, and it was the opinion also of an overwhelming number of people who were citizens of the countries in Latin America. To collect bad debts, the armed might of the United States was brought into use. When force is employed, it is inevitable that somebody is going to be deprived of his freedom; so it was that in the name of a Doctrine upholding freedom, the United States destroyed freedom and gained the terrible reputation of being the enemy of liberty! Small wonder that many an American boy, as he patrolled the coastline of a neighboring republic in a warship or kept guard in the streets and along the docks of a Latin-American city, was confused, as were many of his countrymen at home.

What was it all about? Who was right? Who was wrong?

The countries of tropical America—those lying along the coasts of the Caribbean and on its islands—have the reputation of being langorous paradises washed by blue seas beneath lovely blue skies. This is partly true. The beaches, the seas, the emerald forests, the rustling palms and the broad fields of sugar cane all smile and drowse beneath the warm sun.

But there is violence in these lands too. Hurricanes of incredible ferocity, heat, crashing tropic rains and searing trade winds during the dry seasons often turn these paradises into nightmares.

The peoples of these lands, and their politics, are just as turbulent and mercurial as the climate. They have known little of the stability and peace which are so necessary for progress and well-being. Since the times of the earliest Spanish conquests, life for master and slave, for rich and poor alike, had too often been one crisis, one bloody upheaval, after another.

Citizens of richer, more orderly countries tend to think of Latin-American wars and revolutions as comic opera affairs. The actors are supposed to parade about in glittering uniforms; guns are supposed to be shot off into the air or at a donkey or two, never at the other actors. Nothing could be further from the truth.

In the long history of man on earth there have been a

good many vicious and bloodstained dictators. Latin-American countries, especially those lying in and along the Caribbean, have seen more than their share. The revolutions which brought them to power have not resembled comic operas. The regimes which these vultures set up have been as ruthless and brutal and cruel as any that men have ever inflicted on their fellows.

The island of Santo Domingo had such a background. Santo Domingo was shared by two "republics"—the Dominican Republic and Haiti. The history of each is typical, and so is the series of circumstances which invoked the Monroe Doctrine and the interference in their internal affairs by the United States of America.

In the year 1904 the people of the Dominican Republic were more than weary of confusion and turmoil. There was one question at the moment on everybody's mind—rich planter on his big estate and dockworker in a city slum. Was the United States going to do anything about the problems which plagued the country? Because of the recent stand which America had taken on similar problems in Venezuela, this was not an unreasonable question for people to ask. Many of them were so sick of the confusion that they desperately wanted *somebody* to step in and straighten out the mess. They wanted Big Brother to do something.

Since gaining its freedom from Spain, the Dominican Republic had known very little beyond fighting and power struggles. First one faction was up, then it was down and another took its place. The situation which came to a head in 1904 started with a revolution which brought an especially violent dictator to power in 1886.

Ulises Heureaux was as brutal and bloodthirsty and greedy a man as ever lived. In the years he ran the country he brought it the first stability it had ever known—but at what a price! He ran the nation as though he owned it lock, stock and barrel. He mortgaged it, its people, and its future in any way he saw fit. Those who protested were murdered. Before he was finally eliminated he had butchered some 2,000 of his fellow citizens and had run up about $20 million in debts contracted in Europe and in the United States.

Heureaux was assassinated in 1899 and from then until 1904 the Dominican Republic was shaken and torn by one gory revolution after another. All the "outs" who had been without power for so long wasted no time trying to get their hands on the reins of government and, in traditional style, into their country's cash box.

Matters finally reached such a horrible state that even the various quarreling groups sensed that something had to give. An ex-priest named Carlos Morales was accordingly chosen as a compromise President. Almost immediately he found himself in deep trouble.

A number of European creditor nations announced intentions of using armed force to collect the money due them. Just how much sympathy they deserve is a matter of question. The Dominicans claimed that the interest rates were exorbitant. They said their country had not even received all the money which was supposed to have been lent it. In addition, they said, the funds which had arrived had mostly fallen into the hands of the defunct dictator Heureaux and his henchmen. Very likely there may have been justification for all these compaints, but that didn't help Morales. At best his position was shaky, and if he were to be thrown out of office, there was little doubt that European soldiers would be landing on Santo Domingo.

In the face of this, Morales appealed to the United States

for aid. Some accounts say that the Yankees didn't need any invitation, but regardless of what triggered the action, President Theodore Roosevelt acted with his usual speed. America would lend a hand!

A treaty was worked out with the Dominican Republic. The United States was to take over the main source of revenue—the customs—and make definite arrangements to start paying off the clamoring European creditors.

The United States Senate must ratify all treaties, and accordingly this one was submitted to the Senate. In the accompanying statement, President Roosevelt said, "Either we must submit to the likelihood of infringement of the Monroe Doctrine or we must ourselves agree to some such arrangement as that herewith submitted. . . . We are simply performing in peaceful manner . . . that international duty which is necessarily involved in the assertion of the Monroe Doctrine. . . . This in reality entails no new obligations upon us, for the Monroe Doctrine means precisely such guarantees on our part. This protocol affords a practical test of the efficiency of the United States Government in maintaining the Monroe Doctrine."

And this, in a nutshell, is the famous Roosevelt Corollary of the Monroe Doctrine. It meant that the United States had to assume control of its erring neighbors and make them behave. Either this, or make no protest when other nations might seek to untangle the muddled affairs. It was this Big Brother–Little Brother relationship, as well as further extensions of the idea, that kept the United States in hot water in Latin America for so many years.

The Senate would have no part of this treaty. It refused to ratify it, even in the name of the Monroe Doctrine. In order to block the arrival of troops from Europe in Santo Domingo, Roosevelt had to make do with what is called in diplomatic language a *modus viviendi*—a way of living, a way to get along under a temporary arrangement.

America, peacefully, took over the collection of customs in the Dominican Republic and started making payments to the treasury of the country—45 percent of everything collected. The rest was divided among the various creditor nations. The arrangement worked beautifully. The American officials were honest and efficient. The threat of foreign armed intervention vanished, and more cash, even under the 45 percent division of duties, flowed into the government strongboxes than it had when the Dominicans themselves were doing the collecting. In addition to this, literally for the first time in centuries, the country was peaceful. The reason for this was that the "outs" no longer had access to funds collected at the customs houses and so were unable to finance their revolutions.

However, by 1911, this happy state had come to an end. President Caceres was assassinated and new disorders set in. Greed, lust for power and personal ambition once more were rampant in the Dominican Republic. America continued to pay off the foreign creditors, so the likelihood of European intervention was gone, but this didn't stop the Dominicans from killing and stealing from each other. After all, 45 percent of the money was going into the treasury, and with the duties honestly collected this was quite a huge sum. Public debt began to build up again, along with the suffering of the common people as the different groups which came to power squandered gigantic sums on military equipment which they used in efforts to keep themselves in control.

There was no doubt that further action was necessary, not to protect the country from foreign soldiers but to protect it from its own citizens! The United States had to take the next step, and it was logical and inevitable in the light of those already taken. When the current Dominican Government refused to accept reforms, American Marines landed in 1916. A full American military government was proclaimed, with absolute control over all expenditures and the collection of all revenues—internal as well as those at the customs houses.

The United States had indeed come a long way in its application of the Monroe Doctrine. It is very easy to say that America had no business doing what she did, and yet under the circumstances it would have been difficult to have done otherwise.

The Dominican Republic now enjoyed a peace and a prosperity such as it had never known. Schools, roads and harbors were built. An efficient army and civil service were trained. At last it seemed that perhaps the Dominicans were learning something of the responsibilities of citizenship in a democracy and something of the larger blessings that would come in due course with the acceptance of such responsibilities.

American Marines were withdrawn in 1924, and the affairs of the country returned to its own people. The Dominican Army, trained by U.S. Marines, managed to keep order until 1930, when President Vasquez attempted to get himself re-elected, illegally, to the Presidency. Thereupon the Commander of the Army, General Rafael Trujillo, saw to it that *he* was elected. Under his absolute dictatorship, the nation continued to prosper. In 1940 the last aspect of American intervention—the collecting of customs duties—was withdrawn and the Dominicans were in full control of all their national affairs. By 1947 Trujillo's government had paid off the last of the foreign creditors in full, and the Dominican Republic was solvent and on its own feet.

Siberia
ARCTIC CIRCLE
Arctic Ocean
Bering Sea
Beaufort Sea
Alaska
ARCTIC CIRCLE
KODIAK ISLAND
54° NORTH LATITUDE
CLAIMS PRIOR TO 1812
CLAIMS FROM 1812-1823
Pacific Ocean
SITKA
AS A RESULT OF THE MONROE
RUSSIAN CLAIMS WERE CONFINED
NORTH OF 54° NORTH LATITUDE FROM
QUEEN CHARLOTTE ISLANDS
54° NORTH
VANCOUVER ISLAND
PRESENT U.S.-CANADIAN
The Extent of Russia's Claims
SAN FRANCISCO
FORT ROSS
The Sea Otter

Except for the sad fact that democracy didn't exist at all with Trujillo lord and absolute master, it might have been thought that finally the nation was on the road to responsible and honorable self-government.

Alas, debt was more easily eliminated than the old disease, dictatorship. Trujillo's "subjects" finally tired of him. He was assassinated in 1961, and the troubles in the Dominican Republic began all over again and continue to the present day.

There are those who say that President Theodore Roosevelt inaugurated "dollar diplomacy." He did not. His actions might have been hasty or undiplomatic when he authorized intervention in the Dominican Republic, but they were not taken for the primary purpose of collecting anybody's debts. No American President ever cared less about collecting debts for anyone—American or European—than Roosevelt. What he did care about was the security and well-being of the United States. He felt that European troops on Santo Domingo would have jeopardized this, and he acted as he did because of this concern, under the flag of the Monroe Doctrine.

Perhaps American intervention in the Dominican Republic was necessary and justified; perhaps it was not. The point will be argued for a long, long time. Intervention in Nicaragua was something else, and it was this "extension" of the Monroe Doctrine that ushered in the hated era of "dollar diplomacy." This episode *was* a bill-collecting expedition. James Monroe would have turned over in his grave had he known to what purposes his patriotic and honest sentiments of 1823 were put.

Like that of most of its sister republics, little Nicaragua's history had been one of bloodshed, revolutions and crises as various strong leaders dominated it. Over the years, bankers, big corporations and international financial adventurers of one sort or another had slowly managed to lend Nicaragua more and more money and to acquire more and more control over its life.

The trouble which ended in American intervention started in 1909, during the administration of President William Howard Taft. There was no doubt no American dishonesty was involved, but there were enough interested people in high places to cause wonder. For example, President Taft's brothers owned shares in one of the companies which had large financial stakes in Nicaragua—companies which would have been in grave danger if the country had a dictator hostile to their interests. As events unfolded, this never happened. And the reasons it never happened were strong ones—the United States of America, the United States Marine Corps and the Monroe Doctrine.

From 1893 to 1909 Nicaragua had been ruled by a grasping and conquest-minded dictator named José Santos Zelaya. Zelaya had no special love for the Yankees, but he was very partial to Yankee dollars! Over the years Zelaya granted many concessions to American businesses. These concessions were tremendously profitable to him, and to them. Certainly nothing could beat the profits to be taken from an entire country, though small, if it were controlled from top to bottom, from one end to the other.

Trouble started when Zelaya took steps to pay off the debts which his country owed by borrowing additional money in London. He planned to oust the Yankees and substitute Englishmen, probably pocketing a very sweet percentage from the process for himself.

The Yankees had no intention of letting this come to pass! It would be a violation, to say the very least, of the current convenient interpretation of the Monroe Doctrine.

A revolution broke out in Nicaragua against Zelaya, and there are those who say that it was instigated by Americans. When Zelaya executed two American soldiers of fortune, Washington broke off diplomatic relations with him, sent warships to Nicaraguan waters and landed two hundred Marines at Bluefields, the principal port. These ships and Marines prevented the importation of guns and ammunition needed by the Nicaraguan Government and were directly responsible for the success of the revolt against Zelaya.

The new administration was "friendly" to America, to put it mildly. A treaty was signed, and Nicaraguan customs were placed in the hands of Americans.

When President Taft presented this treaty to the Senate of the United States for ratification, he said, "A further responsibility is thrown upon us by the Monroe Doctrine. Much of the debt of Nicaragua is external and held in Europe, and while it may not be claimed that by the Doctrine we may be called upon to protect an American Republic from the payment of its just foreign claims, still complications might result from the attempted forced collection of such claims. . . ." And so on and on!

As with President Roosevelt before him, the Senate refused to ratify the treaty. And like President Roosevelt, Taft was willing to settle for a *modus vivendi.* By 1912, the European debts were all repaid—re-financed by Americans who now controlled Nicaraguan banks, railroads, mines and big agricultural enterprises. American business was running the nation, and there was no other way of looking at it.

Unfortunately, this happy state of affairs was endangered when Nicaraguan citizens launched a real revolt. Colonel

Butler landed with 2,000 tough, well-armed Marines, and through revolution and unceasing turmoil, they were in Nicaragua until 1933. During all this time, however, the investments were in no danger.

When the Marines were finally withdrawn, it was thought safe to do so because they left behind them a highly trained army of Nicaraguans in complete control. Throughout all the years of the occupation various Nicaraguan patriots fought the Americans bitterly, as well as the various "puppet" dictators the United States supported. The most famous of the Nicaraguan freedom fighters was General Agusto Sandino. He successfully defied the Marines and is regarded with high esteem in the annals of the Marine Corps. He was a hard, tough, skillful opponent.

The name of Sandino is also extremely famous all over Latin America for quite another reason. He is remembered as a man and a patriot who struggled against Yankee Imperialism and all that it represented—including the by now despised Monroe Doctrine.

With variations, the same story unfolded on Haiti, the other "republic" on the island of Santo Domingo. Here, the United States acted in the role of spanking a very naughty little brother and possibly, in the light of what was going on, had some reason to do so.

To say that politics in Haiti were chaotic is something of an understatement. Perhaps of all Caribbean countries, the history of Haiti was the most confused, the bloodiest. "President" followed "president." Some of them lasted less than a year. The regime of each seemed more cruel and savage than that of the one before. Worst of all, these revolutions never seemed to be uprisings of the Haitian people themselves, but were conducted by professional killers, highly trained armies of mercenaries who sold their services to the aspirant for power who bid the highest. And the bids were high, because whoever was in power, even though for a brief time, had complete freedom to loot the national treasury.

By 1915 affairs in Haiti had degenerated into pure savagery. The dictator at the time, Guillaume "Vilbrun" Sam, in an effort to suppress a revolt against him, had arrested all suspects, likely or not, and thrown them in prison. Then he simply murdered them all in cold blood. *Now*, a popular revolt took place. Sam was captured and his body hacked to pieces. The limbs and torso were dragged through the streets in an orgy of blood and released hatred. The unhappy nation was sinking rapidly down into primitive bestiality.

On the next day United States Marines landed, and the occupation, which began under President Woodrow Wilson, lasted until 1934. Haiti at last knew peace—of a sort. Over the years there is no doubt that Haiti's economy and general well-being improved immensely. The foreign debt was being paid off as usual, and roads, schools, harbors and business were on the upswing under honest American administration.

But there was no liberty on Haiti. Marines and native soldiers under their command killed thousands of Haitian revolutionaries. Many of them were the hated mercenaries, but many also were honest citizen patriots fighting for freedom.

America justified intervention for the customary reasons —foreign debt, chaotic political problems. To these had been added the additional and perhaps most important reason of all—a desire to end the bloodshed. After all, no one stands by and refuses to "interfere" as his nextdoor neighbors go after each other with axes. The catch, however, was that all this was done in the name of the Monroe Doctrine, which made it a more and more hated thing throughout Latin America. In the minds of people who had to begin with perhaps no great love for fact, and certainly no great love for the United States, it became the very tool of Satan himself.

And now, as a result of the intervention in Haiti, on top of the dubious reasons for the "big stick" policy, the spirit of the Monroe Doctrine had been even further perverted. The United States not only had the right and duty to interfere in the affairs of its Latin-American neighbors, it had a monopoly to do so. For example, other nations had occasionally offered to help in troubled areas by sending troops along with those of the United States. This was particularly true in the case of Haiti, where human self-respect and compassion made the presence of armed forces necessary to bring the butchery to a halt. The civilized world truly was appalled at the bestiality; it needed to be stopped, and other nations were willing to help. French marines actually were landed at Cap Haitien. But the United States would have none of it! The Monroe Doctrine would not permit it. Thus America was not only the policeman of the hemisphere, but its judge and jailer as well.

The growing fears of Latin-American peoples were not calmed by additional incidents. Just before World War I, for example, in 1913, President Woodrow Wilson openly called for the overthrow of Dictator-President Victoriano Huerta in Mexico. The reason? Huerta had come to power through revolution! United States troops for a time actually occupied the Mexican port of Vera Cruz, to the disgust of all of Latin America.

The distrust of Latin America for the United States was clearly shown by the attitudes of many of the countries during World War I. In spite of great cultural ties with France and sympathy for her plight, only eight nations, half-heartedly, declared war on Germany. Of these eight, seven were pretty much dominated in one way or another by the United States or by Great Britain. Seven others—including the larger and more powerful states, such as Argentina, Chile and Colombia—remained neutral. America's nearest neighbor, Mexico, was to a large extent pro-German.

13

SO IT WAS that for an exceedingly complex variety of reasons, the United States became deeply involved in the affairs of many other Western Hemisphere nations for more than thirty years over the first part of this century. The causes were many—attempts or supposed attempts by European nations to collect debts, insistence of American financial interests that their investments be protected, and sometimes even the name of humanitarianism. American intentions may have been good or they may have been selfish, but the fact of America's actions was there for the whole world to see. These actions did the country little good.

As far as the reactions of Americans at home were concerned—well, the people were simply too busy with their own affairs. To the man in the street, these various interventions were not especially popular, but then he didn't know too much about what was going on. Unless he was very rich and had money invested in Latin America, or unless he happened to be in the Marines and was exposed to some very sticky and dangerous jungle fighting, the average American really wasn't much concerned.

The Monroe Doctrine was something he had heard about and learned about in school and believed in, but after all, his opinion was apt to be simply that the countries where America had intervened "never had it so good." In a sense he was right. Order was maintained. Bills were paid. Debts were honored. Schools were built and so were roads, harbors and railways. Sanitation was improved and real progress made to eliminate such maladies as yellow fever and malaria. Maybe even, hopefully, America's neighbors to the south would learn to take care of their affairs as they should. If the average man in an average street in America had been polled, this would have been the general opinion about what was going on in these rather outlandish little "republics" in Latin America.

Many people in the United States, though, were genuinely confused and disturbed at these applications of a hallowed doctrine, particularly since this doctrine was originally supposed to have been the champion of freedom. In spite of the confusion and some real dismay, however, the Monroe Doctrine became more solidly a part of American thinking than ever—both public and official. If anybody had thought about it really hard, he would have concluded that this was a very strange situation. Believing in freedom, the country had drifted into a position where it denied freedom to others whenever it saw fit to do so.

This two-faced point of view led the nation into some very peculiar situations. For example, after the United States had "intervened" and played a vital part in helping to win the first World War, fear of violating the Monroe Doctrine played an important part in America's rejection of the League of Nations after the war. The country was afraid it might become involved in European squabbles! Even though President Wilson insisted that a special exception be made in the Covenant of the League for affairs which might be covered by the Monroe Doctrine, the Senate refused to go along with him. America never did join the League.

As the years passed, the need for "dollar diplomacy" and "big stick" intervention in Latin America became less and less. Interference by European nations in the Western Hemisphere became more and more unlikely. Much of this was due to the fact that many of the nations of Latin America were maturing and were managing their affairs better, although this maturing process too often appeared to take the form of efficient military dictatorships. In spite of the continual militarism, however, many of these governments and peoples did seem to be settling down and slowly but surely turning more and more to responsible, democratic government.

The total effect was that America's "imperialistic" activities ceased and the Monroe Doctrine became less the strong cornerstone of the country's foreign policy. It was a long way from being dead, though! As the 1930s rolled along, the Monroe Doctrine was revived, revealing that it was just as strongly engraved on American thought and emotion as ever. And, just as important, it proved itself to be just as flexible and adaptable to new interpretations as ever.

Beginning with the term of President Franklin Delano Roosevelt in 1932, a new and entirely different extension of the Doctrine came to life. It ceased to be a principle which covered unilateral action on the part of the United States alone. Evolving along an entirely different path, the principles of the Doctrine became instruments of cooperation. They became the shielding umbrella under which hemispheric solidarity was achieved against a common enemy.

"The essential qualities of a true Pan-Americanism must be the same as those which constitute a good neighbor—namely, mutual understanding and, through such understanding, a sympathetic appreciation of the other's point of view. . . . The Monroe Doctrine . . . was and is directed at the maintenance of independence by the peoples of the continent. It was aimed and is aimed against the acquisition in any manner of the control of additional territory by any non-American power."

These were words which President Monroe would have understood. They stated clearly and simply what he had been talking about more than a hundred years before. They were spoken by President Franklin D. Roosevelt in a "fireside chat" in 1933, as he launched the famous Good Neighbor Policy.

The whisper of trade winds, the click of maracas and the tinkle of marimbas had sounded many a sour note over the years, but they began now to play a happier tune. As the United States started to practice what it preached, Uncle Sam began to emerge in a new light. His neighbors to the south came to realize that "The Colossus of the North" was possibly not the grasping ogre he had seemed so many times in the past. Under the Good Neighbor Policy, he started to act like a good neighbor instead of a policeman.

Upon request, technical assistance in a multitude of ways was made available to America's neighbors in Latin America. Manufacturing of all sorts, medicine, highways, bridges, schools, fisheries, aviation and agriculture all benefited by American know-how and substantial financial assistance when it was necessary. Cultural relations blossomed as music, art, dancing, poetry and literature flowed back and forth. North Americans learned much they had never known of the beauties, history and romance of Spanish America. South and Central Americans, on their part, began discovering a great deal that was exciting and vital and beautiful in the bustling giant of the United States. Latin America had traditionally been oriented to Europe in many ways, but now, under the stimulus of the Good Neighbor Policy, its peoples began turning their eyes northward.

The changes were long overdue. The abuses of the clear and high principles expressed in the Monroe Doctrine had at times almost made a mockery of them. Protests and complaints from Latin America had never ceased, and more people at home also clamored for an end to the hypocrisy. From as far back as the administration of Calvin Coolidge in the 1920s, the thinking American gagged at the pretentious doubletalk and the two-faced application of the principles expressed by James Monroe. These principles were good and honorable; America had with reason taken them to its heart. But it was becoming weary of their perversion and use to ends for which they had never been intended. People were beginning to realize that unless the national security were truly in danger, the United States had no business, all on its own, interfering in the private affairs of its sister Western Hemisphere nations. If conditions were so bad now and again in some of these nations that something had to be done about them, then clearly the remedy should be a joint effort.

In various hemispheric congresses and conferences, in the public mind and in actual practice, the Roosevelt Corollary of the Monroe Doctrine eroded away. American Marines were gone from Nicaragua by 1933, from Haiti the following year. By the time the Inter-American Conference was held in Buenos Aires in 1936, the United States was ready to join other nations in declaring such intervention illegal. The agreement was ratified unanimously by the Senate. This action possibly was the first time in history that a mighty nation, such as the United States, willingly put its signature to a document which limited its powers so drastically.

Still to come, however, were even further changes and extensions in the idea and spirit of the Monroe Doctrine. They were brought about mainly by the spreading threat of totalitarianism. "Today Germany, tomorrow the World." Such was the boast of the Nazi regime of Adolph Hitler, and it was echoed just as arrogantly by his Fascist partner in Italy, Benito Mussolini.

These two 20th-century European dictators seemed well on their way to making good their brutal plans. The weapons had been tested and sharpened in the Spanish Civil War of the mid-1930s, when their interference resulted in the downfall of the Spanish Republican Government. By 1940 France and most of the rest of Europe was overrun and only England continued to resist, fighting for her life alone and shuddering under ceaseless bombing.

Hitler and Mussolini, like so many Old World conquerors of the past, turned their eyes westward, particularly to Latin America. The plum which dangled before them was indeed tempting. Raw materials, vast empty spaces, food in abundance seemed ripe for seizure by the strong. Germans and Italians had been emigrating to the countries of Central and South America for years. For the most part they had flourished and were relatively unassimilated by the native populations. Bunds, fifth columns, and various other Nazi and Fascist organizations maintained the spirit and the discipline and the aggressive philosophies of their homelands.

Axis (for so was the connection between Rome and Berlin called) businessmen sought trade advantages and at the same time conducted outright espionage upon their hosts. Most of the airlines which crisscrossed Latin America were controlled and operated by Germany. Import businesses, exports, manufacture, agriculture and many other industries were operated by Germans and Italians in line with the philosophies of Hitler and Mussolini and without consideration for the governments or peoples of their adopted countries.

In addition, Nazi and Fascist penetration of Latin America was assisted by a further sad fact. Many native-born citizens of these lands—themselves not German or Italian—were potential dictators, and they found in these totalitarian concepts much they could understand. They dreamed and plotted for the day when they could throw off the restricting processes of democracy and set up tight Axis-type governments. The situation was so explosive in many Central and South American republics that Hitler boasted he could take any of these nations simply by picking up the telephone and giving the word for action to his primed and ready countrymen and their well-organized native sympathizers.

A beginning had been made to combat this swift-growing menace at the 1936 Buenos Aires Inter-American Conference. Resolutions were passed which stated that "in the event of an international war outside America, the New World Republics would consult together as to the necessary steps to be taken." As the threat of war in Europe loomed closer, many further conferences adopted additional measures, all of which tended to make security a mutual responsibility of the various nations.

At the same time, all these steps and measures slowly but surely made a hemispheric doctrine of cooperation and unity out of the Monroe Doctrine. Just prior to the Japanese attack on Pearl Harbor, Hawaii, on December 7, 1941, this had gone so far that at a meeting of the American states held in Havana, Venezuela proposed a resolution which stated flatly "that any attempt on the part of a non-American state against the integrity or inviolability of the territory or the sovereignty or the political independence of an American state shall be considered as an act of aggression against all the states which shall sign this declaration." The resolution was adopted.

This high-sounding and impressive statement was soon put to the test of war. Nine Latin-American nations promptly declared war on the Axis after Pearl Harbor, and eventually all severed relations with it. This was in direct contrast to the lack of interest and cooperation at the time of the first World War. The Latin-American nations were not able to contribute greatly to the war effort in munitions or in fighting men, but in a multitude of other ways their assistance was invaluable.

The United States and her allies were permitted to establish air, submarine and other naval and military bases wherever they were needed. The enormous natural resources of Central and South America were at the disposal of the United States, and the list was impressive, particularly as it included many of those essential raw materials which had been lost to the Japanese. Manila fiber, rubber, kapok, quartz crystals, copper, tin and cinchona bark—from which the vital quinine, so necessary to combat malaria in the South Pacific, was made—constituted only a small part of the materials supplied by Latin America.

Last, and possibly most important of all, was the fact that in one way or another most of these countries managed to purge themselves of the spies, the highly dangerous fifth columns and the saboteurs. That the United States was able to be relatively free of such menaces in her own back yard was a tremendous contribution to the war effort and can never be underestimated.

The war was finally over when Japan, the last Axis partner, surrendered on August 14, 1945. Peace at last had returned to earth. Amidst the general rejoicing, Uncle Sam and the Señorita had the chance to take a good, fresh look at each other. They were pleased by what they saw. Although, as in all families or neighborhoods, there had been quarrels and misunderstandings, the time now seemed appropriate to bury the hatchet once and for all. The nations of the New World set about seriously to see what could be done to make life better for all concerned.

In continuing meetings after the war, the positions taken by various American diplomats—both North and South American—invariably were such as to draw everyone in the New World closer and closer together. The horrible image of the United States, the brutal giant with octopus-like tentacles, changed. The feeling was that perhaps even the Monroe Doctrine—"Monroeism," as it was called—could be made to work for the benefit of everyone.

One thing gradually became clear. The world seemed to be lining itself up after the war for a new series of power plays, and no one in North or South America wanted any of the new global alliances or treaties to be of greater importance than the regional agreements which had been hammered out, after so many years of misunderstanding, by the nations of the Western Hemisphere. Uncle Sam and the Señorita liked their arrangement and wanted nothing to interfere with it.

People have complained that these inter-American agreements of cooperation and consultation have internationalized the Monroe Doctrine to the point where it has no more real meaning for the United States. This is not true.

Each nation under its protective umbrella, including even Canada and Greenland during the war, has the right to act quickly and individually if its security is threatened. This applies to the United States as well as the others. The Monroe Doctrine has been strengthened and given much more validity in that its "internationalization" commits many nations to act with and for each other. These are not mere words. During the war, hemispheric defense, which is the heart of the Monroe Doctrine, was a common problem. It was faced together, and acted upon together, with courage and speed. The defense of the principles of liberty was shared.

Latin-American realization of the terrible threat of world-wide communism—a new kind of dictatorship—seems in some ways to have been ahead even of North American awareness of it. This was clearly demonstrated during the deliberations which established the Charter for the United Nations in San Francisco.

As a result of the determined and insistent stand taken by Latin-American Republics, Article 52 was inserted in the Charter. It states that nothing in the Charter must rule out the existence of regional agreements and agencies. What was meant, in essence, was that no one could have the right to rule out the Monroe Doctrine as it was now practiced and understood as an instrument of hemispheric solidarity. There must never be a Soviet veto of the principles laid down so long ago by James Monroe.

In 1948 Uncle Sam and the Señorita took their final vows when the OAS, the Organization of American States, was brought to life in Bogotá, Colombia. The Constitution of the OAS first defines the hopes and the dreams and the highest aspirations of mankind. It then resolutely sets about spelling out how these great precepts might be achieved in the Americas.

The roots of the OAS go far back into the history of the New World, clear back to Simón Bolívar's call for cooperation when he asked for a hemispheric meeting in Panama in 1826. With true prophetic vision, Bolívar realized the need and the advantages of a community of New World nations.

From 1826 to 1890 many Inter-American conferences were held, some of them in Latin America and some in the United States. They were not true continental meetings, however, as not all of the nations attended. Many subjects were covered in these meetings, and sincere, but fumbling, efforts were made to reach agreements on such widely separated matters as mutual defense, international law, extradition, copyrights and the practice of such nonpolitical professions as medicine.

In 1890 the first true International Conference of American States was held in Washington, D.C., at the invitation of the United States. It continued to operate through a permanent bureau from quarters erected in Washington and was known from one end of the Americas to the other as the Pan-American Union.

Through regular meetings and through its activities in the field, the famed Pan-American Union contributed much to the sense of community and to the welfare in general of all the American states. Matters of culture, sanitation, boundaries, patents, finance, trade and many others were improved through efforts of the Union. Thus it was that in spite of selfishness, greed, lack of understanding and "Monroeism," efforts had been made over the years toward a greater unity in the New World. It took the terrible agonies of World War II, however, to produce a generation of citizens of the American republics absolutely determined to accomplish something concrete, especially in matters of mutual security.

In 1947, a formal Inter-American Conference for Maintenance of Continental Security and Peace was held in Rio de Janeiro, Brazil. This conference was the eleventh full-scale congress convened by the American states since the formation of the old Pan-American Union back in 1890. The delegates in Brazil drew up and adopted a pact for common protection against aggression, known as the Rio Treaty for Reciprocal Assistance. It stated in formal and binding terms the principle that an attack against one American state would be considered as an attack against all.

So it was throughout all the years, all the ups and downs, the wars and the hatreds, the dream of an organization of American states had never died. Out of this dream over the passage of time much good had come. The hope for peace and for all the things of peace had prospered. Most of all, and before anything else could be done, the climate for a sense of continental community had to be created, for only out of this feeling of solidarity could spring the determination and the means to keep the peace.

Elaborate machinery has been set up to help the OAS in its work as guardian of the peace. For example, in any dispute—and there have been many of them—at least one of the parties involved *must* request OAS help before intervening or taking armed action. Run of the mill squabbles are handled by a permanent council. In more serious cases the council may summon a meeting of OAS Foreign Ministers. Any OAS decision reached by two-thirds vote is binding.

The OAS has performed valiant service in its role as an expanded, many-nation enforcer of a "hemispheric" Monroe Doctrine. It has "interfered" many times in the affairs of its fellow New World nations, almost always with success.

Individual member nations of the OAS—Costa Rica, Nicaragua, Ecuador, Peru, the Dominican Republic and others—have had their guns spiked by visiting peace teams and the weapons at their disposal. These weapons are powerful—ranging all the way from public censure, up through sanctions of many kinds, to actual joint armed intervention when all else has failed in troubled areas.

No one knows whether these quarrels would ever have become so serious that the United States, on its own, would have intervened under some new extension or interpretation of the old Monroe Doctrine. This never became necessary. The problems were resolved by cooperative OAS action.

14

AT A MEETING OF THE OAS held in Caracas, Venezuela, in 1954, a growing and extremely dangerous threat to the peace of the Western Hemisphere was on everyone's mind. As though girding for struggles to come, the community of American states pinpointed the threat, brought it clearly into the open and took steps to prepare for the future. This new danger was international communism.

One of the basic tenets of communism is that it must be worldwide in order for its success to be assured. In line with this, after the establishment of a Communist regime in Russia in 1917, the leaders of this particular brand of dictatorship have sought in every possible way to interfere in the political lives of other nations, and by whatever means necessary to overthrow the established governments and impose Communist-type governments in their places. Latin America has had its share of such attention with the result that Communist parties have flourished there. In a number of countries they are important and wield much influence.

There are many very complex reasons why communism

has achieved the success it has had in Latin America, but in general there have been two major themes upon which agitators played.

The first is the truly pitiable condition in which vast numbers of people live in Latin America. The almost feudal situation of millions of city slum dwellers and the nearly slave-like existence of equally numerous Indians, miners, plantation workers and peasants living deep in remote countrysides provided the classic opportunity for the sowing of communism, with its false promises of quick relief. What these ignorant, exceedingly oppressed *pelados,* or "peeled ones," as they are called, did not know was that their traditional masters—the military dictators, the land-owners, the mine-owners and others—would merely be exchanged for another set of dictators, Communist-style. The sad part is that the call to revolt, to change, was offered by the Communists in the name of freedom. Since for many of the victims of Communist propaganda almost anything would have been an improvement, many of them believed.

Nor was Communist influence confined solely to the poor and oppressed. Converts were made in other segments of the population as well, as, for example, in the ranks of young students and university graduates. These young people found that democracy, as it was practiced, offered them few opportunities. Their hard-earned education did them little good unless they belonged to, or had connections with, the established, well-to-do families that controlled the economic life of their homeland. These youngsters had ambitions; there was work which needed to be done—businesses to be opened, raw materials to exploit, living conditions to be improved. Little of it was possible as long as the lands, the resources and the peoples were under the hard control of foreign investors or the equally tough domination of home-grown financial and military dictators. As in the case of the terribly poor, the false promises of communism seemed to offer quick relief, and many became converts.

The other theme, which in a way bolstered the first—the lack of opportunity—was that of still smoldering anti–United States feeling. The support by the United States in the past of Latin-American dictators, the memories of "dollar diplomacy" and of Monroeism in general and the occasional greed of American businesses made it possible for the basic truths to be twisted. All troubles could be blamed on the United States, and this feeling could be turned by Communists so that America was painted as the arch-enemy of progress, the uncompromising enemy of freedom, the "capitalistic ogre."

The knowledge that true democracy and true freedom can be obtained only by honorable acceptance of the responsibilities which go hand in hand with liberty is a hard and often unpalatable concept. For many people in Latin America who had known only lack of opportunity, dictatorship, political irresponsibility, poverty, hunger and oppression, it was too sophisticated a concept. They were ripe for any change that would better their conditions; it was easier to listen to the rosy but false promises of communism than it was to face up to the hard truth.

The future of democracy, and of freedom in Latin America, depends upon the speed with which truly grave social injustices can be cured. They can be cured only by the untiring and unselfish efforts of true champions of freedom. Democratic groups in Latin America, and their number is very great, are cleansing their countries of the old evils. To do this they are receiving the help of the great democratic power to their north—the United States of America. Succeeding American administrations are cooperating and furnishing this aid in ever-increasing amounts. The Alliance for Progress, formed during the administration of the late John F. Kennedy, is an example of such cooperation.

Meanwhile, there are serious and immediate problems. The OAS is meeting them as best it can. In 1954, for example, it became painfully apparent that Guatemala was falling under the control of a Communist-type government. Large shipments of arms from behind the Iron Curtain were in the country and in the possession of local Reds. Obviously communism would soon pass from the talking stage to the shooting stage. A meeting of the OAS was called, but no positive action resuulted. Only a counter-revolutionary movement by Guatemalan exiles, supported by the United States, drove the Communists from power.

In the case of Cuba, the situation was far more critical and far more dangerous.

The long history of Cuba has been filled with violence and bloodshed, perhaps more so than any other Latin-American country. The island, the lovely "Pearl of the Antilles," has traditionally been the gateway for conquest and expansion in the New World. Spain's European wars overflowed with a vengeance to Cuba. It suffered widespread destruction over and over again as the English, the Dutch, the French and even rapacious, free-booting pirates made it the target for ferocious attacks.

Nor had Cuba been able to free herself and become independent from Spain as the other Spanish colonies did. The same reasons existed for independence, but owing perhaps to the fact that Cuba is an island, no help was readily available from the outside. Spain apparently learned nothing from the loss of her other colonies, and in Cuba the graft and oppression increased.

Occasional revolts were put down with incredible ferocity, and the island remained in a continual state of turmoil. In the mid-1800s, several "piratical" expeditions from the United States which attempted to free Cuba were defeated. These expeditions were mainly instigated by proslavery people in America who had in mind to set up more slave territory to offset the increasing antislavery sentiments in the United States. Presidents Franklin Pierce and James Buchanan even made unsuccessful attempts to buy the island from Spain.

War broke out again in full force on Cuba in 1868. It was to last for ten long years and was one of the bloodiest ever fought in the Americas. Over 100,000 Cubans and Spaniards died in this war. It ended by Spain promising sweeping reforms; but as usual, the promises came to nothing.

By the end of the 19th century the Cubans were once more in full revolt against Spain, which sent huge armies to put down the rebellion. In 1898, after the American battleship *Maine* had been blown up in Havana harbor, the United States entered the war. In a few months it was over and Cuba was free. The American occupation lasted until 1902, at which time Cuba was really, and at long last, on her own.

Cuba's troubles were far from over, however. Revolt followed revolt in the typical pattern as one strong man after another sought to rule. The country did not know true democracy, except perhaps during brief periods between the rules of various tyrants.

Throughout all the years of Cuba's history, the country had had close associations with the United States. American citizens had for years been involved in one way or another with Cuba, and Cuban citizens with the United States. The American Government mediated many times in periods of trouble. American soldiers died in defense of Cuban aspirations. American medical efforts made Cuba the most healthful of all Latin-American nations. American support of Cuba's sugar economy helped make Cuba prosperous and enabled the people to build schools, roads and harbors. And Cuban citizens always looked for and found sympathetic help in America. Many expeditions of Cuban exiles trained and launched counterattacks against dictators in their homeland from American bases. Cubans instinctively turned to America, more so than to any other Latin-American nation. The straits between Cuba and Florida are narrow; the traffic across them had always been heavy and two-way.

By 1957, the current Cuban dictator, an ex-sergeant named Fulgencio Batista, seemed to have reached the end of his regime. For many years the unhappy island had been under his rule. Opposing Batista was a bearded revolutionary named Fidel Castro.

In 1959 Batista fled the island and Castro was in supreme control. Cuba, and the United States, rejoiced. Perhaps this new liberator would bring about democracy. In a very short time, though, Castro revealed himself a liberator of a different hue. If not an outright Communist, he was certainly completely and directly under the influence of Communists.

He held no elections. He instigated bloody purges of political enemies. He confiscated private property held by Americans, Cubans and citizens of other countries. He whipped up public feeling against the United States and in many ways was successful in reviving the old cry of "Yankee Imperialism."

In his early days Castro claimed he did not represent international communism, but rather an innocent variety of home-grown socialism. He had every right to do this, and because of the corruption and the heartbreaks which Cuba had endured throughout many years of so-called democracy, no one could blame the Cubans for trying socialism. There were dark clouds, however, even during the early years of this socialism. Castro's desire, so he said, was to rid his country once and for all of the burden of the Yankee economic oppression under which Cuba was allegedly groaning. A good many American "dollar diplomacy" chickens came home to roost. Not only in Cuba but in many other Latin American states, people believed Castro. Officially and unofficially, many were glad to see at least one Latin-American country take steps to get rid of the Yankee "octopus." In Mexico, for example, President Lopez Mateos said that he could not see how Castro was a threat to the peace of the hemisphere.

Not everyone felt this way, of course—in Cuba especially. Once again the traffic across the water between Cuba and Florida revived. This time it was one way, as thousands upon thousands of Cubans fled the tyrant, seeking refuge in the United States.

The United States retaliated against Castro's abuses through economic sanctions, principally against the importation of sugar. This really hurt Castro, since the economy of the island was based upon a thriving sugar industry.

Castro now revealed himself for what he really was. There was no longer any doubt about his Communist affiliations. He delivered Cuba outright to Russia in return for economic aid, armaments, technical assistance. Almost before anyone knew what was happening, the New World had a full-fledged Russian puppet on its front doorstep—complete with Russian citizens and Communists from

China, Yugoslavia and other Iron Curtain countries, all of them happily "helping" Cuba and enjoying the sunshine and learning the rumba!

One inevitable and most ominous development began almost immediately with the Communist takeover in Cuba. The island became a center for Communist agitation throughout all the Americas. To it came hopeful Reds for training and indoctrination. From it were exported agents, spies, arms and explosives to the great plantations, the factories, the city slums and the mines in many Central and South American nations. Poverty, lack of opportunity and all the other things which had always been a very real part of Latin America's troubles provided vulnerable targets for Communist propaganda.

When President Lopez Mateos of Mexico said that Castro was no threat to the peace of the Western Hemisphere, he added that "his country had no obligation to help the United States enforce the Monroe Doctrine." This was the first time in many years that any important official had used the words "Monroe Doctrine." The last time had been in 1933, by President Franklin D. Roosevelt. Since then, during all the negotiations and arrangements for cooperation and security, the words had not been mentioned. Everybody knew the connection, but "Monroe Doctrine," or "Monroeism," brought up too many distasteful memories for all concerned.

The next mention of the Doctrine came, oddly enough, from Soviet Russia! A Russian reporter asked Nikita Khrushchev to give his opinion on the contention that the ultrafriendly relations between Russia and Cuba constituted a violation of the Monroe Doctrine. The Russian Premier was happy to oblige. Among other things, he delivered the verdict that ". . . the Monroe Doctrine has outlived its time . . . has died, so to say, a natural death.

Now the remains of this doctrine should best be buried as every dead body is buried so that it should not poison the air by its decay."

In answering this blast, the United States did not doubletalk. The State Department said that "the principles of the Monroe Doctrine are as valid today as they were in 1823 when the Doctrine was proclaimed. The principles which the United States enunciated in the face of the old imperialism to intervene in the affairs of this hemisphere are as valid today for the attempts of the new imperialism. It consequently affirms with vigor the principles expressed by President Monroe."

In view of the risks and the still smoldering resentment of Latin America toward anything which smacked of the old "Monroeism," the Doctrine was not invoked in Cuba. Beyond economic sanctions, the administration of President Eisenhower did little beyond trying to arouse opposition to Castro through the OAS. Nothing happened. Too many influential Latin-American states were still not convinced of the presence of any danger. Among them were Argentina, Brazil, Chile, Mexico, Bolivia and Ecuador.

When John F. Kennedy assumed the duties of President, continued attempts were made to awaken Latin America to the danger and to provoke united action. Still the OAS could not decide.

One aspect of the impending crisis took place in 1961. The President of the Revolutionary Council of Cuban refugees in the United States announced that armed forces were being landed in Cuba to overthrow Castro. The invasion was a failure, but the part which the United States is said to have played—not in the landings themselves but in their organization—is still open to world-wide criticism. This invasion was the famous "Bay of Pigs" fiasco.

Shortly afterwards, President Kennedy made a strong

statement for the record and also as a warning. He said, ". . . our restraint is not inexhaustible. Should it ever appear that the inter-American doctrine of noninterference merely conceals or excuses a policy of nonaction—if the nations of this hemisphere should fail to meet their commitments against outside Communist penetration—then I want it clearly understood that this Government will not hesitate in meeting its primary obligations, which are to the security of our nation. Should that time ever come, we do not intend to be lectured on 'intervention' by those whose character was stamped for all time on the bloody streets of Budapest."

During all the talk and all the palaver over Cuba, there was one place where the fateful words "Monroe Doctrine" were used. This was in the United States itself. If Latin Americans were not alarmed over communism in Cuba, North Americans were. They dusted off their most precious statement of policy from the past to voice their alarm—the Monroe Doctrine. Over and over, in committees, in newspapers, in unofficial quotes by official people, by political figures and, most of all, by ordinary citizens in the street, fear, anger and alarm over this "violation" of the Monroe Doctrine were expressed. In times past the words of the Doctrine had often been twisted and confused. People had been divided on just how they should be applied or interpreted. Now there was no confusion. People knew *exactly* what James Monroe had faced and what he had in mind, and under the banner of his words, modern Americans wanted something done.

But Fidel Castro continued on his way, never seriously molested in his "socialization" of Cuba. On October 22, 1962, the fiction ended. The entire situation changed overnight.

In an address to the nation, President Kennedy announced that air patrols over Cuba had discovered the presence of Russian war missiles capable of delivering atomic warheads anywhere in Central America or along the east coast of the United States. Bases for longer-range missiles, able to strike any part of the Western Hemisphere, were well along in construction.

The President did not hesitate. He had already directed American armed forces to institute a blockade of Cuba by air and by sea. He said, "It shall be the policy of this nation to regard any missile launched from Cuba against any nation in the Western Hemisphere as an attack by the Soviet Union on the United States, requiring full retaliatory response upon the Soviet Union."

Thus President Kennedy spelled out to Cuba and to the Soviet Union not only what the response of the United States would be but also an expression of solidarity among New World nations. There was no mistaking the meaning of such words. Their intent was clear, as was the full awareness of what Castro's socialism was.

Kennedy also laid the matter before the United Nations and called for emergency consultation meetings of the OAS. This time there were no dissenters. The rattle of nuclear missiles was audible from one end of the Western Hemisphere to the other. There were no agonized cries of "Monroeism" or "Yankee Imperialism." The OAS to a nation endorsed the quarantine of Cuba. But it was too late. Castro had been allowed to go too far. Cuba was no longer a battlefield for the various "isms" of native tyrants, or even for honest patriots on fire with the delusion that the United States was their mortal foe.

Cuba was a missile base—an armed and cocked Russian missile base. Russian ships bringing long-range missiles were already on the high seas. While the whole world watched with horror, these vessels steamed closer and closer, bearing their awesome cargoes. What would happen when they met the blockading American ships?

What happened was important. Khrushchev backed down. He turned his ships around and headed them for home. He also agreed to withdraw the short-range missiles and the long-range bombers from Cuba. He may have thought the Monroe Doctrine dead and better off buried, but it had proved to be a very lively corpse. Never in the history of the United States had the principles of James Monroe been so powerfully affirmed. Never before had America mobilized soldiers or sent ships to sea and planes into the air—with weapons primed and loaded—in defense of those ideals. It is true that at other times America had taken up arms over those ideals, but always in more complicated, roundabout and perhaps even questionable ways. It remained for Soviet Russia to challenge directly the Monroe Doctrine—and be answered directly.

During all the furor and danger, the words "Monroe Doctrine" were not used officially. They were shouted from one end of the country to the other by the people, but they did not appear elsewhere. Perhaps America was learning tact; the government, without weakening its stand, hadn't tried to cram them down anybody's throat. It is also interesting to note that America had acted *unilaterally*—that is, on its own, thus giving the lie to those people who said that the country had negotiated itself out of this right.

Again, in 1965, another case arose where America had to act unilaterally in order to get something done. This time the crisis was in the Dominican Republic.

Castro had continued to export communism, supplied in almost every case with trained agents, arms and propaganda. Revolts and discoveries of Communist plots flared throughout the hemisphere. They were all handled in one way or another by the different countries involved except in the Dominican Republic.

Early in the year an uprising took place against the tyrant then at the head of the government. To the world it looked like just another internal power struggle. By May of 1965, however, this was seen not to be the case. Various revolutionaries *were* trying to control the country but at the same time, Castro Communists began to take over. They did this by taking advantage of the general turmoil.

Quickly the United States was confronted with an agonizing situation. Unless something was done right away, the Dominican Republic would turn into another Cuba, another Communist satellite. Before this could happen, President Lyndon B. Johnson dispatched armed forces to the island. The United States was once again back in the business of "intervening" unilaterally in the affairs of its neighbors.

The OAS was notified about the danger, but immediate action had to be taken; otherwise the Dominican Republic probably would shortly be a Red-controlled nation. The OAS finally took action, and soon there were troops from other Latin-American countries trying to help those from the United States prevent the formation of a Communist government.

Later, in explaining why he acted as he did, President Johnson stated what some people have come to call a "Johnson Doctrine." The term is incorrect. More properly, what he enunciated was simply another interpretation or extension of the Monroe Doctrine. It is a corollary of the Doctrine, aimed at the prevention of "the establishment of another Communist Government in the Western Hemisphere." Also, along the same lines as President Kennedy during the Cuban crisis, Johnson said, "I want you to know and I want the world to know, that as long as I am President of this country, we are going to defend ourselves. We will defend our soldiers against attackers. We will honor our treaties. We will keep our commitments. We will defend our nation against all those who seek not only to destroy the United States, but every free country in this hemisphere."

The times were different, the peril was different, but the cause was the same. It was the cause of freedom—freedom for the United States and freedom for the Western Hemisphere. Lyndon Baines Johnson spoke the words in 1965, but the meaning was the same as in the times of James Monroe in 1823.

15

THUS, IN 1823, and in the present day as well, the Monroe Doctrine has been and is, first, last and always, a statement of self-preservation, a statement of dedication to the enduring principles of liberty—even though it has been twisted and turned and occasionally used to cover situations in ways which were not to the honor of the United States or in the true cause of freedom.

It has been examined and dissected, praised and condemned by all manner of people—men in the street and politicians in high places—domestic and foreign. The words of the Doctrine are not, as many fiery sword rattlers insist, blind dogma. If violations of the principles are alleged to have taken place, this does not mean that America must spring to arms, taking instant action. Each set of circumstances is different. The nation can choose or not choose, as seems expedient, to invoke the Doctrine. It can be applied or not applied, as seems proper at any given moment.

Whether the Monroe Doctrine is ever invoked again by name or otherwise, Americans know what it means. It will never be forgotten as long as they believe in the ideals upon which the United States was founded. The chances are that in the future, as in the past, whenever the political morality of any other nation is such as to jeopardize these ideals, Americans will come to the quick conclusion that the best defense of freedom is an offense based on the principles so clearly outlined by James Monroe.

Perhaps the old expression of the plain Americans in the street, the shop, tavern or farm back in 1823 still expresses best the nation's feeling: "If they'll leave us alone, then we'll leave them alone. If they don't, then we'll have to do something about it."

The Monroe Doctrine can best be described as a "state of mind" rather than a set of rules governing American conduct. This state of mind could be called by its narrow and shortsighted term—isolationism—but it is much more than this. It is a state of mind built upon self-interest, but more nobly and broadly, it is a state of mind built upon the hope and dream and ideal of freedom—not simply freedom for citizens of the United States of America, but freedom for all men, and justice and honor and opportunity for all men.

The difficulty now, as it was in 1823, and as it has been throughout all the years between, is to determine where the true cause of freedom lies. Freedom's banner, as well as those of oppression and tyranny, attracts all manner of men, ready to use the ideal for their own selfish ends. Perhaps the real test of whether the drums beat for freedom or for a false image is a very simple one: do men groan under a burden of oppression inflicted upon them by their fellow men, regardless of cause or the reason given? If they do, then they are not free and their problem inevitably must become the problem of freedom loving peoples everywhere. This is because no man may enjoy freedom, or long remain free, nor may any nation, if their neighbors are slaves. Tyranny is a cancer which spreads without regard for boundaries.

Men are born to be free. Only as free beings can they reach full flower, know their greatest fulfillment. President Monroe and his advisers in 1823 knew this full well. They believed idealistically in freedom for all men, and they also were highly practical—they knew that unless the nations of Latin America were also free, there could be no enduring liberty for the United States. To this end they were prepared to tempt the future; they were prepared to warn the great powers away and to "isolate" themselves from the turmoils and quarrels of the Old World. They were willing to risk everything and face up to what possibly would have been a disastrous war over what they knew to be right.

This interlocking necessity for freedom for all men is infinitely more acute today than it was in 1823. And infinitely more difficult is the task of deciding what is the true cause of freedom. The enemies of freedom are more powerful than ever before. Their disguises are more subtle, their weapons stronger. They have learned how to dominate other men's minds and spirits as well as their bodies. And above all, infinitely more distant are the battlefields where freedom's enemies must be met and more dangerous is the course for those who challenge the tyrants.

If the enemies of freedom are vastly more powerful than in the past, so too are the weapons of those who believe in freedom. Freedom too is strong and vital, and as always there are brave men willing to risk everything and take up arms in her defense.

The Doctrine of James Monroe has again, today, been expanded to meet the conditions of today's changing world. Not just in Latin America, but in the farthest corners of our earth, men cry out against oppression. The cry must be answered or the liberty of men everywhere will eventually be lost. There is no new interpretation of the Monroe Doctrine to rally men to action today. Only the location of the action and its application are new, and it might be called the "Corollary of 1967." No matter what his face, the enemy is the same as it has always been—oppression.

A Secretary of State, Elihu Root, once said that "it is well understood that the exercise of the right of self-preservation may, and frequently does, extend in its effect beyond the territorial jurisdiction of the state exercising it. . . . It is the right of every sovereign state to protect itself by preventing conditions in which it will be too late to defend itself."

This was said in 1914, and Elihu Root no doubt was referring to the possibility of the use of American armed force in Europe in World War I to prevent the spread of that war and the possible consequent destruction of freedom in the United States. Today's tight, complex world demands similar vigilance. Not just armed forces but other weapons as well must be used against those who would destroy freedom. Even more care must be used to identify the tyrants. Freedom's enemies are not just bombs or cannon, or Nazism or communism. They are all those things which make the minds and spirits of oppressed people receptive to the lies and the false promises of those who would enslave them. The hard truth is that these things must be fought wherever they are found, not just within a nation, or at its borders, or in a hemisphere, but all over the world.

As the areas and the scope of man's ancient fight for freedom have expanded, so have the numbers of people involved. Freedom is everybody's business. Here in the New World it has never been better expressed than by Luis Muñoz Marín, the former Governor of Puerto Rico. He said, "There are great struggles under way in the world, and I believe we should be in position with proper instruments in the Organization of American States to prevent communism from moving in."

The business of upholding freedom in the Western Hemisphere is not just the responsibility of the United States. The nations of Latin America realize this, and it is evident in the changes which have been made in the OAS. One of the big troubles with the OAS, for example, is that it relied too much on meetings of the Inter-American Conference, which are held only once every five years. Emergencies in between are handled by the Foreign Ministers who assemble only *after* a problem arises, and often this is too late.

Today steps are being taken to strengthen the OAS and to make it more responsive, capable of taking quick, decisive action as a situation demands. At a very recent conference in Rio de Janeiro, important steps were taken in this direction to make the OAS faster-moving, with less talk and more deeds. These changes provide for frequent top-level meetings, a streamlining of the OAS charter, incorporation of the Alliance for Progress into the OAS and increased cooperation on the economic front.

All such proposals no doubt will bring forth agonized cries of objection from many North and South Americans. The proposals *do* tend to strengthen hemispheric solidarity at the expense of national sovereignty. This cannot be helped. The world has become too small, and too dangerous, ever again to permit a rampant and selfish nationalism to run wild. Aggression, oppression and the curtailment of freedom in the most remote spot—regardless of boundaries or outraged superpatriots—cannot help but bring suffering to all.

And there are still some, but fewer, cries of "Yankee Imperialism" from south of the border. The vast masses of the peoples in Latin America are genuine believers in democracy. They realize that Communist penetration is a real danger and not just an imaginary foe conjured up by the United States to further selfish plans of its own for colonialism. And lastly, they realize that the struggle in defense of freedom against communism is one for the entire hemisphere to tackle jointly. It is too big for any one nation to handle, and has to be fought on too many fronts.

For these reasons, slowly but surely, the Organization of American States is being strengthened. So it is that now *all* peoples of the New World who cherish freedom are coming to accept the full and honorable commitment which was first pledged openly by President James Monroe in 1823. This pledge has to be reinterpreted again in the "Corollary of 1967" to meet the needs of today's rapid and complex times, but the commitment is the same as it was in 1823.

It is the commitment of men of honor everywhere to defend their own freedom, and that of all other men, wherever they may be. Monroe's Doctrine has survived the years because it speaks of truth, because what it says is as meaningful now as it ever was for men who believe in liberty.

Additional Reading

Esler, L. A. *Presidents of Our United States.* Chicago: Rand McNally & Co., 1935.

Perkins, Dexter. *A History of the Monroe Doctrine.* Boston: Little, Brown & Co., 1963.

Green, Constance McLaughlin. *Washington—Village and Capital, 1800-1873.* Princeton, New Jersey: Princeton University Press, 1962.

Rothery, Agnes. *Washington Roundabout.* New York: Dodd, Mead & Co., 1942.

Murdock, Myrtle Cheney. *Your Uncle Sam in Washington.* Washington, D.C.: Monumental Press, 1948.

Leeming, Joseph. *The White House in Picture and Story.* New York: George W. Stewart, Publisher, Inc., 1953.

Thomas, David Y. *One Hundred Years of the Monroe Doctrine.* New York: The Macmillan Co., 1923.

Donovan, Frank. *Mr. Monroe's Message.* New York: Dodd, Mead & Co., 1963.

Gilman, Daniel C. *American Statesmen—James Monroe.* Boston: Houghton Mifflin Company, 1883.

Index

About the Author

Paul Rink is a native Californian, born in San Jose on January 6, 1912, and now living in Monterey with his wife and two children. He majored in literature and science in college, and has been an engineering officer in the Merchant Marine and on other ships. He lived in Panama for seven years where he engaged in the import-export business; was an engineer for the Panama Canal; served in the U.S. Embassy. During all the years of work, travel and study, Mr. Rink wrote continually, and his articles have appeared in national magazines. He has also worked in the documentary and semi-documentary field in TV and is the author of several books for young people.